HOW TO LAUNCH A
BRAND

By Fabian Geyrhalter, FINIEN

Brandtro Publishing
320 Pine Avenue, Suite 1010
Long Beach, CA 90802

Ordering Information:
For details, contact the publisher at the address above or
send an email to orders@brandtro.com

Brand Atmospheres is a registered trademark of Geyrhalter
Design, Inc., DBA FINIEN.

ISBN 978-0-9896461-3-0

Dedication

This book is dedicated to the
entrepreneurial innovators
and Fortune 500 disruptors who
believe in change by design.

Table of Contents

01

02

03

04

FOREWORD

This book will guide you through the steps necessary to build a brand from the ground up. Most entrepreneurs, even seasoned brand managers, launch first and then work on slowly transforming the new offering into a brand. A logical progression, I would agree. After all, how can you possibly launch as a brand if you don't have any customers or marketing outreach and—obviously, since you just launched a new offering—you have no legacy or advocates?

The simple answer is *by design*. Design relates to the systematic process you have to adhere to, which is likely the primary reason you are holding this book in your hands. In addition though, design truly holds the key to the success of your new brand. It will set your offering apart to look, feel, and sound like a brand at the time of launch, as opposed to something that might or might not have the power to eventually turn into a brand. This book will teach you how to launch your brand by design.

What does it even mean to be a brand today?

"The word 'brand' needs a re-branding—due to its brand longevity the brand legacy is not brand-correct anymore." I heard myself say these words unexpectedly in an interview one day, but they had been on my mind for a while. This comes as no surprise, as I probably use the word at least one hundred times a day in the course of running a brand consultancy. The word gets tiring, especially as it leaves a bad aftertaste and I feel the need to first

convince people that it is not a bad term before I use it any further. *Brand* is not a four-letter word.

Despite the negative connotations associated with the term, branding is more important today than it has ever been before. It is not only consumed, but also created and curated by the masses through their very own personal (public/social media) brand. Brand is alive and kicking, and though we will not be able to change the term, we can change the perception away from the logos of luxury goods (e.g., Gucci, Chanel) and larger-than-life corporations seen as evil-doers (e.g., Exxon, Walmart) to a modern necessity. If created and nurtured in an honest and authentic way, "brand" can be turned into the holistic "aura" of a product or service provider (or person) that we are allowed to have admiration for (e.g., iPhone), aspiration towards (e.g., a nonprofit organization), and sometimes draw inspiration from (e.g., TED Talks). It is time to define the word brand, specifically for new ventures: What does it mean to be an early stage brand?

BRAND IS A SERVICE, PRODUCT, COMPANY, OR PERSON WITH

SOUL THAT IS ATTRACTIVE & SMART

| THE BRAND PLATFORM | THE BRAND ATMOSPHERE | YOUR BRAND'S USABILITY |

1. Soul is the beating heart. It is the reason a company should exist and also the reason that your initial attraction matures into love. You put your trust in brands with a soul—and often your money follows soon thereafter. Not much different than with human relationships, soul is the reason why we care for each other, or a particular brand.

2. Attractive is the brand aura, the emotional connection you feel when you come into contact with the brand. It is the design and the voice that are carefully created and curated over time in a consistent and particular manner.

3. Smart is its usability. How easy is it to engage with the product or service? For the tech industry, excellent user interface and user experience are essential; for consumer products, quality packaging design and superior product are vital; and for the service industry, the design of key offerings often determines whether a brand is "smart."

Now that we have discussed the complex strategy that creates the beautiful simplicity that makes a brand, do you think that perhaps we should give the word another chance?

So much of the world of branding is about creating a specific perception. I won't guide you to fake it—I want you to make it. Like most guidebooks, *How to Launch a Brand* will work only if you apply it in a truthful and consistent manner while working with your team and extended partners. On the following pages, you will learn how to oversee the brand launch process, from laying a stable foundation by creating a "Brand Platform," crafting a memorable name, to building a meaningful identity design, and, finally, applying that vision to cohesive consumer touchpoints.

This book encompasses two decades of brand-building experience across all varieties of verticals, which I have distilled into 109 easily digestible pages. I can assure you that it will pay off instantly as you approach your next—or very first—brand launch. It will be challenging at times and always educational, but most importantly, it will be a highly rewarding experience when you know the steps necessary to succeed. The next pages will teach you these steps and enable you to form a rich, inventive, unique, cohesive, and satisfying brand.

Once you launch, please send me a note. I want to learn how the book helped you and your team or where I can improve it; like a brand, this book is a focused yet ongoing work in progress. Its second edition has been guided by readers' feedback and knowledge gained in the interim.

Fabian Geyrhalter

The Brand Development Process

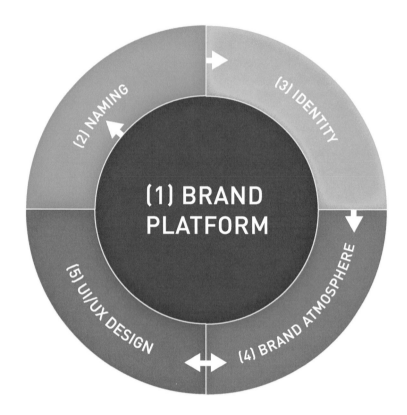

The chart above shows the five major steps you need to take to get from vision to successful brand creation. Starting with a solid Brand Platform, this process is designed to keep you focused as you develop the critical components of an extraordinary brand.

STEP 1

Create a Brand Platform*

STEP 2

Devise a brand name

STEP 3

Design your brand's identity

STEP 4

Craft your Brand Atmosphere Touch Points**

STEP 5

Develop your brand's Web presence**

*If you are a tech startup with UI/UX design at the core of your emerging business, begin website wireframing and prototyping (step 5) while you develop your Brand Platform. This will give you time to make sure your digital product aligns with your brand strategy.

**Steps 4 and 5 can be handled in tandem to save weeks of valuable speed-to-market time. Because technologies and approaches change rapidly, step 5 is not included in this edition of the book. To learn more about this subject, download our free white paper by visiting http://tinyurl.com/FourPhases.

Resources for Getting Prepped

Selecting the Right Agency Partner

Before delving into the how-tos of a brand launch, it is important to understand who you need to surround yourself with to succeed during the brand creation phase. If you would like guidance on selecting a creative agency or deciding whom to include in your new brand's entourage, download this white paper: *http://tinyurl.com/AgencyPartner*

Gaining Stakeholder Buy-In During the Early Stages of Brand Creation

Just as "no man is an island," no entrepreneur should exist in a vacuum. We naturally seek the advice of our coworkers, friends, family, and mentors. Validation and constructive criticism are crucial in developing a brand. However, one can easily upset this delicate balance by either ignoring the counsel of others or seeking everyone's opinion. This step in the process is a rather slippery slope, but we have devised some tips and tricks to save you time, money, and sanity. This white paper is available at *http://tinyurl.com/StakeholderBuyin*

BRAND PLATFORM

A Brand Platform is a layered and interconnected web held together by a core of company values. This chapter will help you understand the what, how, who, and all-important why of your brand.

Font: Hermes

01: BRAND PLATFORM

Think of your new brand as a building. The Brand Platform is the foundation upon which the construction takes place. If the foundation is strong and well considered, anything built on it has a higher chance of being equally sturdy. Too often, new brands rush to create a company name and visual identity before having a firm Brand Platform in place, essentially putting a beautifully designed cart miles before the horse. Before your chosen design firm begins any work, you want to have a keen understanding of your new brand's benefits, marketplace, target audience, and personality.

A good Brand Platform addresses all of these areas, assessing every aspect of and association within your future brand. The platform contains both the tangible (e.g., the selling points of a product) and the intangible (e.g., the attitude of the brand). Working systematically, a Brand Platform explores all of these areas, culminating in a holistic portrait of your brand-to-be.

A strong Brand Platform is the foundation for a strong brand. It serves as a guide for developing the brand's identity, consumer relationships, and marketing. The stronger the Brand Platform, the stronger the brand. One of the most identifiable brands of the past decade is Apple Inc. The company's voice is clear, consistent, and compelling. It has legions of devoted fans who happily brave the elements just to purchase the latest Apple product. It has a distinctive personality: innovative, sexy, geek-chic, and rebellious. All of this is the result of the identity design, product design, and advertising campaign built on a brilliantly engineered Brand Platform.

Leadership expert Simon Sinek explains Apple's success in his TED talk entitled "How Great Leaders Inspire Action." Sinek argues that Apple has the same access to technology, talent, agencies, and media as its competition. What sets Apple apart is the foundation upon which the company is based. Where most brands explain what they do and how their product differs, remarkable brands go one step further—they tell the audience why their brand exists. In the case of Apple, it is the following: "We believe in challenging the status quo. We believe in thinking differently. The way we challenge the status quo is by making our products beautifully designed and user friendly. We just happen to make great computers." This level of communication connects with the audience on both an emotional and a logical level, thus relating to the consumer's psyche.

BUSINESS PLAN VS. BRAND PLATFORM

It is important to make the distinction between a business plan and a Brand Platform. Although a business plan does not have a specific format, it typically lays out a company's goals and strategy over a set period of time and will include an assessment of projected earnings. Conversely, the key objective of a Brand Platform is to clearly define a company's target audience and formulate a brand persona that will speak directly to that audience. This book assumes you already have your business plan in place, but don't worry if you don't—a Brand Platform can often significantly change or influence the business plan.

A Brand Platform is a layered and interconnected web held together by a company's core values. This chapter will help you understand the what, how, who, and all-important why of your brand by presenting examples of successful (and not-so-successful) brands. You may be able to tackle this process alone (within your firm or with your partners), but this process is best orchestrated and vetted through a brand consultant or firm.

DEFINING A BRAND'S POSITIONING

What makes your brand unique? Why will consumers be drawn to your product? How does the audience perceive your brand? These critical questions play into your brand's place in the market—its positioning. Concretely defining your brand's position is crucial because it serves as a backbone for developing a business direction, marketing message, and overall identity.

Note that *positioning* is not the same as *concept*. The idea behind the brand is the concept, whereas positioning articulates the benefits to the consumer. You may have the most brilliant idea for a brand, but if you cannot compel the consumer to make a purchase, you have nothing.

The Positioning of a Brand Serves to Define Two Points:

- *What the product does*
- *How the product is viewed by the target audience in the competitive landscape in the short and long term*

Simplistic as it may sound, it can help to think of your brand in terms of *problem* and *solution*. What daily struggle does your brand alleviate? Does your product or service help consumers save time or money? Will it make them feel fulfilled, give them an esteem boost, or provide a noteworthy experience? Put yourself in your audience's shoes: why should they buy into your brand? All positioning falls into one or more of these categories:

- *Functional (solves a problem or provides a tangible benefit)*
- *Symbolic (provides a feeling of belonging or self-image benefit)*
- *Experiential (provides physical or mental stimulation)*

**EARLY PROTOTYPING
FOR TECH STARTUPS**

*If you are a tech startup and the website will represent
your end product, spend ample time prototyping
wireframes prior to or during this discovery phase.*

To read more about app and website design, download our free white paper
at http://tinyurl.com/FourPhases.

The positioning statement, as explained by Geoffrey Moore, provides a clear, nuts-and-bolts description of your brand and should take the following form:

> *"To (target audience), our product is the (category) that provides (functional, symbolic, or experiential benefits) because (support/reasons to believe)."*

It is astonishing that a majority of statements leave out the most essential element: the reason to believe. During our Resonaid™ Brand Foundation workshops, it takes entrepreneurs between one and four hours to get this sentence right. But questioning your brand's reason for being and how you can persuade others to believe in your venture is well worth a few hours of pondering. Samantha Paxson, CMO of CO-OP Financial Services, says: "Crafting this statement creates an enormous amount of clarity, regardless if you are a startup or an ever-evolving Fortune 500. It serves as the foundation to a company or products' true north." Consider this example of a hypothetical positioning statement (inspired by the Whole Foods public mission statement) that could support the Whole Foods brand:

> *To health- and eco-conscious consumers, our grocery stores sell the highest-quality natural and organic products that support vitality and well-being because* **we believe in Whole Foods, Whole People, and a Whole Planet.**

As you can see, the "because" part is what really differentiates most brands on an emotional level while informing the company's brand as a whole (excuse the pun).

BRAND IDENTITY ASSOCIATIONS

Big Mac, magical family-friendly entertainment, Steve Jobs, the swoosh logo.

Each phrase immediately conjures up images of the brand it represents (McDonald's, Disney, Apple, and Nike, respectively and rather obviously). Brand identity is a set of associations the target audience makes with a product that reinforces and deepens the positioning to strengthen the relationship with the product. Consumers' relationships with brands are multifaceted—their interpretations of a brand include many touch points that require consideration.

There are four sources of brand identity associations: Brand as Product, Brand as Organization, Brand as Person, and Brand as Symbol.

> **Brand as Product:** product lines, specific products, their attributes, quality and value, functionality, aesthetics, user personality
>
> **Brand as Organization:** the philosophy of your company, the brand's attitude, scope (i.e., local vs. global)
>
> **Brand as Person:** your brand's character traits and how users view their relationship with your brand; this may be typified by a company leader or spokesperson
>
> **Brand as Symbol:** physical properties of your product—a unique design, identity (logo), advertising campaign, or brand heritage (particularly if you are launching a brand under a preexisting company umbrella)

At this stage of your brand's development, you will find that some areas need to be fleshed out (such as Brand as Symbol). As your brand begins to attain a visual identity, these areas will grow in strength. Using Apple Inc. as a test case, you can see the many areas of possible association within a brand:

> ***Brand as Product***
> iPhone
> Apple Watch

Mac
Very intuitive
Sexy yet geared towards usability
Creative users

Brand as Organization
Design driven
Creative
Cutting edge
"Think different"
Innovative

Brand as Person
Steve Jobs
Responsible for making geeks hip and hipsters geeky

Brand as Symbol
Apple logo mark

POINT(S) OF DIFFERENCE AND BRAND VALUE

Today's consumers have more choices than ever before. When they are looking for at-home entertainment they can pick from hundreds of television channels and online streaming services. When they go shopping at the mall, they have access to hundreds of stores and brands. There are even thousands of toothpaste options on the market. With so much competition, brands need a way to stand out and capture their audience's attention. All a brand needs is one strong point of difference to distinguish it from the competition:

Subway: Subway's sandwiches have less fat than the products of most other fast food providers.

TOMS: TOMS donates a pair of shoes to someone in need for each pair sold.

Smart brands have a unique quality that sets them apart. Bridget Field (Small Business, BC) calls this the "so-what factor." If you're opening a coffee shop, ask yourself, "So what? Isn't there a coffee shop on every

SUCCEED WITH PURPOSE

As the consumer market becomes increasingly saturated with competitive product and service offerings, branding is emerging as a key differentiator for prospective consumers. Thanks to a growing number of digital channels that allow consumers to interact with brands, consumers have the opportunity to be well informed before they make a purchase. The most recent Edelman GoodPurpose study, which "explores consumer attitudes around social purpose, including their commitment to specific societal issues and their expectations of brands and corporations," supports the notion that consumers care about how brands address social issues. Furthermore, the study suggests that social purpose plays a role in consumers' purchasing decisions.

87%
of global consumers believe that businesses need to focus on society's interests at least as much as they do on the businesses' own interests
Source: 2012 Edelman Good Purpose Study

80%
of global consumers think it is important for companies to make the public aware of their efforts to address societal issues
Source: 2012 Edelman Good Purpose Study

71%
of consumers would help a brand promote its products or services if there was a good cause behind them
Source: 2012 Edelman Good Purpose Study

91%
of global consumers would switch brands if a different brand of similar price and quality supported a good cause
Source: 2013 Cone Communications/Echo Global CSR Study

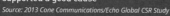

To read more about how to create a brand with a purpose, download our free white paper at tinyurl.com/brandwithpurpose.

corner? What makes my coffee shop different?" Once the difference is clearly communicated to consumers, the brand has a better chance of being selected over the competition. Experts suggest selecting a specific and real benefit over empty, "puffy" claims:

> **A Good Selling Proposition:**
> *"A 10 year bumper-to-bumper warrantee"*

> **A Poor Selling Proposition:**
> *"Quality customer service"*

The first claim makes a specific promise, whereas the latter feels wishy-washy and is easily duplicated by any competitor.

To ensure you differentiate your company from your competitors, make a list of the features and attributes of your service/product. Features refer to specific functionality (e.g., "slip-proof grip"), whereas attributes refer to non-tangible benefits (e.g., "inexpensive"). From there, compare the features and attributes of your brand with those of your competitors in a Venn diagram, noting where you overlap, where your competitors have unique qualities, and where you differentiate:

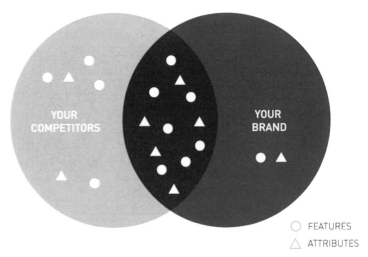

○ FEATURES
△ ATTRIBUTES

Consumers Are Triggered by Emotion Far More than by Logic

Take the example of TOMS. TOMS started out by making trendy and affordable footwear. That's a perfectly good business model. But countless other shoemakers can assert those same claims (e.g., Converse, Keds). What makes TOMS stand out is its commitment to giving back to the global community. The company makes a firm promise: "With every pair you purchase, TOMS will give a pair of new shoes to a child in need. ONE for ONE.®" As a result of this unique perspective, TOMS became the "it" shoe with the socially conscious demographic of Millenials and has seen steady growth since it launched in 2006. Today, TOMS attracts millennials through expanded offerings from coffee to eyewear, all with similar promises.

Another tactic is to fill a void that your competition has overlooked. In the world of soap, Ivory claims to be the best at cleansing, Dove argues that it is the most moisturizing, and Zest promotes its deodorizing capabilities. According to brand consultant Derrick Daye, when Lever 2000 launched, it positioned the brand as the soap "that does it all," thereby making the other products seem incomplete and inferior. At the end of the day, all of the soaps do the same job, but Lever was able to grab a large part of the market by seeing a need and filling it. Why did sales of Lever 2000 skyrocket? Was it because the other soaps were truly inadequate? Or did Lever make an emotional promise: you will smell and look good? Smart brands make an emotional promise to their audience by touting their product's features and benefits. These emotional benefits may include safety, affection, status, self-fulfillment, knowledge, independence, and stability.

THE IMPORTANCE OF CONNECTING WITH YOUR AUDIENCE

You obviously need the consumer to buy into your brand. To reach your specific audience, you need to understand them and know how to communicate so they will listen. Knowing your audience is a critical aspect of your brand's success.

Should anyone ask, "Who is your target consumer?" the answer is never "Everyone." Too often, entrepreneurs make the mistake of wanting to appeal to anyone and everyone. Instead, it is in your best interest to drill down into a specific market. Start by asking yourself, "Who really needs my product or service?" Think about their problems, wants, and needs. As marketing expert David Fry points out, "People don't care about you until they know you care about them."

How does their problem make them feel? Anxious? Unattractive? Left out? Here, Mr. Fry advocates "rubbing salt into the wound"—that is, making them keenly aware of their problem and your proposed solution. Show them how your brand has benefited others and how it bests the competition.

Identifying Your Ideal Consumer

In his memoir and manual *On Writing*, author Stephen King advocates writing for an "Ideal Reader"; King's is his wife, Tabitha. By focusing on one individual, King can ignore the compelling need to please every reader in the world and instead deliver a solid and focused story. Communicating your brand to an audience takes a similar approach. As stated earlier, your brand will never appeal to everyone, but it can appeal to a specific market and enjoy enormous success.

Envision your ideal consumer—the person most apt to be interested in purchasing your product or service. Consider how they are represented in the following demographic categories: gender, age, location, ethnicity, income, education level, mobility, home ownership, marital status, and number of children. An example demographic profile might be *single Caucasian female, middle class, ages 18-24, living in an urban area, college education, no children.*

Of course, not all people in this demographic are exactly the same, and some will not conform to the profile. This is where you will need to consider your audience's psychographic variables by drilling deeper into their personality by considering things such as their values, attitudes, activities, opinions, and anything else you can think of that will narrow your focus. A typical psychographic profile might be *outgoing trendsetter who loves the nightlife, shopping, and fashion; willing to splurge on clothes and cosmetics that make her look her best.*

You can further flesh out your understanding of your ideal consumer by imagining a day in their life: what brands they prefer, whether or not they impulse shop, whether they're bargain hunters or social shoppers, and whether they have any specific interests or family concerns. Creating image boards—"collages" or "mood boards"—of your different target audience personas can help you to better visualize and connect with them.

All products and brands appeal to a niche market. Sometimes the product casts a wide net and captures a "mainstream niche." At others, the audience is more specialized. It may help to think of this in terms of television broadcasting. Very few programs outside of the Olympics or the Super Bowl occupy a "mainstream niche." Yet there are countless

> **> FURTHER READING**
>
> The Number One Most Important Branding Exercise: Don't Think Of Your Audience, Think Like Them
> *tinyurl.com/thinklikethem*

networks and shows that appeal to specific groups; for example, Logo targets the LGBT community and Nickelodeon targets children. The more specifically you understand your niche, the more effectively you can reach that audience and communicate the values of your brand, cementing the relationship between your ideal customer and your brand.

Understanding the Needs of Your Audience

The key to connecting with your audience is understanding what motivates them. As early as 1954, psychologist Abraham Maslow identified five categories of needs (which have remained relatively consistent through decades of revisions). Not long after their initial publication, business strategists and marketers began applying these principles in consumer outreach and advertising. Review the following list of Maslow's needs hierarchy and the brand equivalents, assessing where your offering fits into the system:

Physiological Need
Biological motivators: *food, water, sleep, health, sex*
   Product Examples:
      medicine, health food, bottled water, exercise equipment
   Brand Examples:
      Lunesta (sleep aid): "Leave the rest to us"
      Campbell's Healthy Request (soup): "Heart healthy goes flavor crazy"

Safety Need

Motivated by the desire for *physical safety, security, and stability*

Product Examples:

insurance, safety devices (smoke detectors, helmets), retirement investments

Brand Examples:

State Farm (insurance company): "Like a good neighbor, State Farm is there."

T Rowe Price (financial services): "Invest with confidence"

Belongingness Need

Motives are reflected in *longing for love, friendship, affection, socializing, and acceptance*

Product Examples:

clothing, food, personal grooming

Brand Examples:

Olive Garden (restaurant): "We're all family here"

eHarmony (online dating service): "Beat the odds, bet on love with eHarmony"

Esteem Need

Desire for *self-esteem, status, superiority, and prestige*

Product Examples:

clothing, automobiles, liquor, hobbies, travel, cosmetics

Brand Examples:

L'Oreal Paris (cosmetics): "You're worth it"

Mercedes Benz (automobile): "The best or nothing"

Self-Actualization Need

Motived by the desire for *self-fulfillment, realizing full potential*

Product Examples:

education, hobbies, vacations, sports, museums

Brand Examples:

Weight Watchers (weight support program): "Success Starts Here."

UCLA Extension (extended education): "Explore. Experience. Expand."

Maslow's Needs Hierarchy is a powerful tool to use in determining the efficacy of your brand in terms of audience, business management, product development, visual identity, message, and marketing language.

A clear knowledge of the needs and desires of your target customer allows your brand to connect in a more meaningful and compelling way and stand out in a saturated marketplace.

UNDERSTANDING (AND BESTING) THE COMPETITION

There is an old saying that contends that "forewarned is forearmed," and this saying applies perfectly to understanding your competition when launching a new brand. In their 2007 book *Business and Competitive Analysis: Effective Application of New and Classical Methods*, Craig Fleisher and Babette Bensoussan state, "Most firms operate on informal impressions, conjectures, and intuition gained from tidbits of information." Many new companies fail to thoroughly analyze their competition, whether out of laziness, self-delusion, or simple oversight. To give your new brand the best shot at success, it is crucial that you honestly assess the competitive landscape.

Every brand has competition. No matter how unique your concept is, there will always be something else that is similar. A competitor selling the same product as you (e.g., soap, coffee) is your direct competition. A competitor that is selling a different product but targeting the same audience is your indirect competition (e.g., a bicycle shop, a taxi service, and a car dealer all sell forms of transportation, even if they are very different forms).

"The best offense is a good defense" also applies to knowledge of your competitors. By remaining one step ahead, your brand can exploit the weaknesses of your competition, anticipate their strategies, predict shifts in the marketplace, and thwart threats from existing and new rivals.

Creating a detailed profile of a select few of your rival companies, and even one for your own brand, can help you see how you measure up and where there is work to be done:

Background
Location of headquarters, offices, retail space, and online presence
History of brand, events in brand's timeline, and trends within the company

LAYER OF PROTECTION

Even if branding is mainly about positioning, image, and voice, it provides something of much greater value for new ventures: a thick layer of protection.

With a startup product or service, you may be so intrigued by its novelty or functionality that you decide to make a purchase—if the price is right. With a brand, you fall in love. Love is a strong word. Love does not fade easily. Once you have created love, you will compete on a much higher level—one that is not about price. Your initial customers— the ones you have to fight so hard to gain in the initial months—will quickly abandon ship for a cheaper variation or a competitor's added feature if you did not make a conscious decision to invest both time and money into the process of translating your startup into a brand at time of launch. As you progress through this book, you are already on the right path.

Branding for new ventures is first and foremost about an emotional connection—a strong immediate bond—between product/service and person (the customer). If you make that happen, you can sit back and let the competitors come your way; you are protected.

Business structure, ownership, B2B relationships

Products/Services
In-depth examination of product line(s)
New product launches and success rates
Brand awareness and brand loyalty

Branding
Name
Identity design
Tagline and key messaging
Brand colors
UI/UX

Marketing
Customer base and loyalty
Promotional strategies
Social media presence
Distribution channels, exclusivity agreements, geographic areas
Pricing and discounts

Personnel
Number of employees, key staff, abilities
Management strength and style
Employee compensation, morale, and retention rates

Some of this information may be difficult to acquire, and some may not apply to your particular brand, but the exercise is well worth exploring to begin understanding the strengths and weaknesses of the competition. Even after your brand launches, it is imperative to monitor your competition to note any changes in their messaging and strategy.

Additionally, new competitors will come to the marketplace, and they will also require your attention and analysis. Competitors may come from companies in related industries, companies in other geographical regions, and startups founded by employees from existing companies. The market is primed for additional competition when demand exceeds supply, profit margins rise, growth potential is high, there is little competition, or it is easy to start a brand in a particular field.

CONSTRUCTING A PHILOSOPHY

Why do certain brands connect better than others? Great brands communicate on a deeper level. In *Start With Why: How Great Leaders Inspire Everyone to Take Action,* Simon Sinek advocates that a business should tell the consumer not what it does but why it does it. Giving your brand a voice and ideology creates a stronger bond with the audience. Peer Insight's Tim Ogilvie advises that to attract the best employees and customers, businesses should promote themselves as "a cause—not just a company" (Berger, 2013).

> ### > FURTHER READING
>
> How To Go Against The Grain And Create A Brand That Is Built On Your Undiluted Beliefs
> *tinyurl.com/undilutedbeliefs*

Branding expert Martin Lindstrom compares a brand's story to religious doctrine in his book *Brand Sense: Sensory Secrets behind the Stuff We Buy.* Like the Bible, Torah, or Koran, a brand's story is ingrained in the hearts and minds of true believers, touching on the hallmarks of organized religion: "A sense of belonging, a clear vision, enemies, evangelism, grandeur, storytelling, sensory appeal, rituals, symbols, and mystery" (2005, p. 127). To illustrate his point, Lindstrom points to brands with a cult-like following: Disney, Harley-Davidson, Apple, and Hello Kitty. These brands signify more than a product to the fan: they are a way of life with a resonating philosophy. Human nature compels us to love a good story and makes us hardwired to seek something to believe in and identify with, whether that is religion, politics, or cartoon Japanese cats with bows on their ears.

Each of these brands sells an ethos. For Disney it's about magical entertainment and wish fulfillment, for Harley-Davidson it's about freedom and rebellion, for Apple it's about sleek convenience and geek-chic status, and for Sanrio (maker of Hello Kitty) it's about hyper-femininity and emotional comfort. Looking back on Maslow's

Hierarchy of Needs, it isn't hard to see why these brands are so powerful.

Beyond the remarkable benefit a strong philosophy has for your intended market, it also boosts morale among stakeholders and employees. It engenders loyalty and commitment. Google is a tremendous example of brand philosophy in action. The Google persona is one of hard work, excellence, and silliness. As a result, the company runs the premiere search engine and has its pick of the best and brightest in technology hiring. Google employees are consistently ranked as the happiest, most fulfilled workers in the world (Coleman, 2013).

Chances are that you and your team have already constructed a mission statement for your brand. In an article for FastCo. Design, Warren Berger recommends asking thoughtful questions to arrive at a more meaningful set of values:

Why does this brand exist?

Is there a compelling story behind the brand?

How could your brand experiment and grow, moving forward?

What does the world need that your brand is uniquely able to provide?
(Berger, 2013)

Consumers now want more out of their brands than just products. Let's look at outdoor retailer Patagonia to see this method in action (responses are compiled using Patagonia's public online company information):

Why does this brand exist?

"Build the best product, cause no unnecessary harm, use business to inspire and implement solutions to the environmental crisis."

Is there a compelling story behind the brand?

"Patagonia grew out of a small company that made tools for climbers.

Alpinism remains at the heart of a worldwide business that still makes clothes for climbing—as well as for skiing, snowboarding, surfing, fly fishing, paddling and trail running. These are all silent sports. None require a motor. In each sport, reward comes in the form of hard-won grace and moments of connection between us and nature."

How could your brand experiment and grow, moving forward?

"We know that our business activity—from lighting stores to dyeing shirts—creates pollution as a by-product. So we work steadily to reduce those harms. We use recycled polyester in many of our clothes and only organic—rather than pesticide-intensive—cotton."

What does the world need that your brand is uniquely able to provide?

"For us at Patagonia, a love of wild and beautiful places demands participation in the fight to save them and to help reverse the steep decline in the overall environmental health of our planet. We donate our time, services, and at least 1% of our sales to hundreds of grassroots environmental groups all over the world who work to help reverse the tide."

– From Patagonia's Mission Statement
  (source: http://tinyurl.com/patagoniamission)

DEVELOPING YOUR BRAND'S PERSONALITY

Consumers respond to brands that have a coherent and straightforward message. Equally important to your message is selecting a distinctive voice and persona for your company. The audience demands authenticity, and your brand's voice must be

> **FURTHER READING**
>
> Kill Your Brand In Order
> To Create It
>
> *tinyurl.com/brandobituary*

authentic and transparent. You can achieve this in a number of ways— using a relatable character (Apple's "I'm a Mac" guy), a user's perspective (Ford's "Drive One" campaign), or company personnel (Virgin's Richard

YOUR BRAND CHARACTER

Jotting down a list of adjectives that pertain to the character of your brand can be quite helpful in envisioning your brand as a person. Choose from the following adjectives to help you get started:

Bold	*Innovative*	*Caring*
Helpful	*Mature*	*Light-hearted*
Serious	*Calm*	*Rational*
Adventurous	*Luxurious*	*Witty*
Imaginative	*Humorous*	*Altruistic*
Neat	*Mysterious*	*Tough*
Youthful	*Elegant*	*Rugged*
Dependable	*Warm*	*Sexy*
Friendly	*Healthy*	*Leader*
Authoritative	*Worldly*	*Relaxed*
Quiet	*Glamorous*	*Quirky*
Strong	*Old-Fashioned*	*Intellectual*
Whimsical	*Sweet*	*Clever*
Masculine	*Cosmopolitan*	*Feisty*
Feminine	*Gentle*	*Stoic*
Cooperative	*Humble*	*Spiritual*
Edgy	*Energetic*	*Liberal*
Conservative	*Serious*	*Rebellious*

Branson or Kashi Cereal's use of real employees). Characters give the audience someone to root for and follow (think of the success of Dos Equis's "Most Interesting Man in the World"). In digital and social media, a brand character can gain a devoted following, solidifying the bond between brand and buyer. At fifty-five years old, Mr. Clean exemplifies the importance of a strong brand character with his 21,000—mostly female—followers on Twitter (as of January 2016).

Peter Walshe at marketing research consultancy Millward Brown contends that all good brands have a personality archetype, based on Jungian archetype theory, that falls into one of these categories:

Dreamer: *idealistic, different, creative (Apple, Lego)*

Joker: *fun, playful (Doritos, Arrogant Bastard Ale)*

Seductress: *desirable, sexy (Victoria's Secret, Virgin)*

Rebel: *rebellious, dangerous (Red Bull, Harley-Davidson)*

Hero: *adventurous, brave (Jeep, Nike)*

Wise: *trustworthy, intelligent (NPR, Tesla)*

King: *assertive, in control (Mercedes Benz, Rolex)*

Mother: *generous, caring (Dove, Cheerios)*

Friend: *straightforward, sociable (Target, Zappos)*

Maiden: *innocent, kind (Disney, Crayola)*

Thinking of your brand as a person will help you create an authentic voice that will connect with consumers. Writing a list of adjectives that describe your brand (see previous page) or even imagining that your product is a person and writing an obituary that lists its accomplishments and legacy can be helpful in creating that persona.

DERIVING AND EMBODYING YOUR BRAND'S CORE VALUES

Deriving your venture's core values early on is essential to formulating a strong brand from within.

Imagine your core values displayed beautifully in your company's lobby: Your team will see them every day, and those values should engage and inspire them. At the same time, clients and shareholders should be able to read and agree that your core values actually represent and serve your brand well. They need to resonate across the board. I advise to set out your value statements in three very short and actionable sentences—some of the more universally applicable examples I developed with our clients in the past months are:

CHALLENGE THE STATUS QUO
INITIATE INNOVATION
PROACTIVELY COLLABORATE
ACTIVELY DO GOOD
BE THE EXAMPLE
TAKE SOME RISKS
STRIVE TO MAKE EVERYBODY WIN
NEVER STOP ACHIEVING GREATNESS
PERSONIFY OUR CUSTOMER

It is easy to notice that core values often sound similar, perhaps even a bit generic if taken out of context, regardless of how hard I worked with our clients on crafting them. They often do not feel naturally implementable either. Thus, it's no surprise that they often stay put in a PDF document rather than being embodied by the team.

I gave this issue a lot of thought while striving to create work that is intrinsically embodied by our clients to push their ventures into becoming great brands.

I recommend embodying your core values the same way I would recommend you prepare for a very important presentation: Once you have the presentation deck done and the speaker notes inserted and you start practicing, you will realize that the more you practice, the more you embody the content and overall spirit. Then, on the day of the presentation, if you fully embody the content, you will realize that you could deliver a successful speech even if a major electricity outage hit—in candlelight, without slides, without speaker notes—because you are living the content.

Treat your core values the same way: Try assigning one of your new brand's three core values to each day of the work week, then make it your goal to do something each day that turns the words of that core value into action. It might be a project scope document and you decide to question the status quo and try to turn it into a better product. It might be actively doing good and being an example by staying late to help a coworker meet her deadline.

Examples are endless. Because you only have a few core values, if you start checking one value off the list day after day over the course of two weeks and ask your team to do the same thing, you will quickly realize that you do not have to be reminded about the values anymore—you will just be living them. This will be the magic moment where you will be embodying your brand's core values, and if that neglected PDF were accidentally erased, it would not matter anymore. Action, as we all know, speaks louder than words.

ESTABLISHING YOUR BRAND ARCHITECTURE

Launching a new brand without having a strategic growth plan in place is like launching a kayak into a river without a paddle. You will not be able to forge ahead on a deliberate path without something to guide you. Having a strategic plan for a brand architecture structure can help successfully guide the growth of your company as it expands into a web of brands, either built from the ground up or acquired into your portfolio. Putting a brand architecture structure in place in the early stages of your brand development will help you avoid the following mistakes:

Narrow branding focus: Your branding does not anticipate future directions, and when the time comes to expand, your entire Brand Platform and strategy must be reconsidered. While it may be difficult to predict the growth of your company in these early stages, it is important to avoid trapping yourself in a brand strategy that doesn't allow for future growth.

Misbranding: Promoting a new product or service under an existing brand that does not have the same target audience and/or speak the same language can confuse customers.

Overlap: Having multiple products under different brand identities that fulfill similar needs can be inefficient for your business and make it difficult to build brand loyalty.

On the following pages, we'll explore the two broad categories of brand architecture options and outline the top three things to consider when formulating your own brand expansion strategy.

Strategy Option A: House of Brands

Procter & Gamble, Unilever, Kraft Foods—these are examples of "houses of brands" where the parent brand has multiple sub-brands that each have their own unique brand positioning, marketing budgets, and target audiences. For Procter & Gamble, one of their sub-brands is CoverGirl. The general consumer of CoverGirl probably makes no connection between this brand and its parent company. A glance at its website and packaging doesn't immediately reveal any association between the two companies. You'd have to look closely to find the words "Procter & Gamble" hidden within the fine print.

CASE STUDY

With well over 100 brands under its umbrella, including Jell-O, Capri Sun, Oscar Mayer, Maxwell House, Athenos, Planters, Lunchables, and Kool-Aid, Kraft Foods is in markets around the world. With such a large subset of brands and the need to target consumers in different segments of the market, Kraft's marketing strategy requires different positioning and identity for each brand. For example, Capri Sun, a fruit juice sold in a fun, squeezable package, targets children ages 4–12, while Maxwell House Coffee targets a completely different audience of adults ages 30+. Separate marketing strategies for each of these brands allow them to have clear, undiluted messaging that connects directly with their unique target consumer.

Weighing the Pros and Cons:

+ **Pros:** A house of brands allows for market diversification and creation of messaging specific to each brand's target audience. This is also an easy option for new brands because it takes less planning at the outset of the initial brand creation.

- **Cons:** Each brand must independently build its reputation, which requires extra marketing expenses and individual budgets for each brand. Obtaining unique trademarks for each brand can be an additional hurdle and expense.

When to Use:

Your brands are so dissimilar that they require significantly different marketing strategies

Parent brand legacy is secondary

Product offerings are so closely related that having them under the same brand could lead to cannibalism of sales

Strategy Option B: Branded House

Apple, Intel, FedEx—these are examples of corporations adhering to the branded house model of brand architecture. In this structure, the brand identity mark of the parent brand is carried through to the sub-brands so that there is a recognized relationship between the two in the marketing efforts.

Weighing the Pros and Cons:

+ **Pros:** This strategy builds brand loyalty over time and makes new product launches more cost-effective in terms of marketing efforts because the new product can piggyback on the success of the parent brand rather than having to build its own reputation. Apple is a great example of this: it seems as though it can launch any product and have an immediate fan base because the brand legacy is automatically attached to every new offering.

- **Cons:** A PR disaster at the parent or sub-brand level could have implications for all brands within the portfolio because the relationship of the sub-brands is so intertwined in the mind of the consumer. This strategy has the potential to pigeonhole your business if you want to branch out into different segments.

When to Use:

The brands within your organization can share the same overall brand promise

The parent brand has a strong legacy that the sub-brands can use to their advantage

CASE STUDY

Our client, CO-OP Financial Services, was a strong candidate for the branded house architecture strategy. The company supports a large network of credit unions and offers multiple distinct services and products under its brand. The CO-OP parent identity serves as a solid foundation upon which distinct but cohesive identity variations could be added. This strategy helps members quickly identify CO-OP locations with shared branch or ATM services along with digital products with distinct but integrated brand designs.

Top Three Considerations for Your Brand Architecture Strategy

No one would argue that Virgin (a branded house consisting of ventures in the travel, entertainment, health, and business segments) isn't a financially successful operation, but one can't help wondering whether their marketing would benefit more from a house of brands approach as opposed to a branded house approach. Their rebellious and edgy persona may turn off some audiences when attached to services such as their Virgin Health Bank, "a business enabling parents to store their baby's stem cells."

When starting your new venture (or expanding your current one), it is important to consider the long-term vision you have for your company. This can help determine whether a branded house strategy or house of brands strategy is right for your business objectives. The following are some items to consider when it comes to deciding between a branded house vs. house of brands approach:

Company naming: It is important at the outset of your new venture to choose your company name wisely. If you have any inkling that you may want to expand in the future—specifically into a branded house approach—you need to ensure that your company name isn't too narrowly focused. This was the issue recently encountered by the web-based file exchange company YouSendIt. Once the company realized its name was limiting it in terms of future growth potential, it had to go through the expensive task of renaming its business to Hightail and educating its target audience about the change.

Conversely, Fast Company is an example of a brand whose naming strategy expanded seamlessly when it was ready to create a new network of sub-branded websites in 2009. The additional websites feature content related to innovation in business and technology and are named Co.Design, Co.Exist, and Co.Create. Each site utilizes Co. as a prefix, which is short for "company" as well as "collaborate." Fast Company was able to differentiate its new websites while still establishing a clear connection to the larger brand through naming.

Common messaging among brands: Does the growth plan for your company include products or services that could share the same overall brand promise for your consumer? Starbucks is now carrying a new line of snack bars and freeze-dried fruits packaged under its subsidiary brand, Evolution. In a smart marketing maneuver, rather than packaging the bars under their own brand, Starbucks leveraged the reputation and brand promise of "freshness and quality" that the well-known juice brand has built over its twenty years in business.

Number of companies in your portfolio: While it's not impossible to have a successful branded house approach for a company with a vast number of brands, you run the risk that your messaging will become diluted as your corporation grows. This is where the future vision of your company comes into play—if you foresee large growth and corporate acquisitions over the years, a house of brands approach will provide the most useful strategy for applying unique messaging to each of your brands. If you foresee the creation or acquisition of new brands to be on the more moderate size, a branded house approach can lead to a more easy and cost-effective means to introduce new brands into the marketplace.

Corporate structures and relationships among brands can become increasingly complex over time. To help navigate the growth of your new venture, strategic brand architecture planning can help ensure that you end up with a strong branded house or house of brands (whichever is right for your particular situation) instead of a disorganized and confusing web of companies. Be sure to get assistance from your branding agency or consultant to guide you in everything from company naming conventions to strategic brand identity systems that will have the ability to expand with your company.

Throughout the brand development process, we recommend that you frequently reference your Brand Platform. As the backbone for your brand launch, the Brand Platform should be carefully considered and fine-tuned. Jamie Koval asserts, "A well-defined, easy-to-articulate strategy makes everything intuitive. The attitude, expression, and behavior of the brand simply become second nature inside and outside the organization" (Wheeler, 2013). Once you and your team have arrived at a consensus on the Brand Platform, the next steps in the brand's development will organically fall into place.

BRAND PLATFORM:
Takeaways & Insights

+ While creating your Brand Platform, if you question your idea, scratch it and start over at any point.

+ Think big and think long term. This is the time to create a foundation on which your brand can be built and expanded in the future.

+ Every brand has a sweet spot; try to find yours early on to manifest and expand upon it.

+ Use your Brand Platform as your brand launch manifesto and guide. Share a synopsis of it with your extended team and refer back to it religiously.

+ Positioning and brand personality will define the next steps in the creation of your brand. Pay particular attention to those and embody them along the way.

NAMING

When people ask you what your company or product name means (and they will), make sure it comes with a good story to back it up. With so much competition in the marketplace these days, consumers are seeking more than just a product: they're seeking to connect with your brand on an emotional level.

Font: Rockwell

02: NAMING

The name of your new brand—quite possibly your organization's greatest asset—will usually be with you forever. It will become the launch pad from which all the other elements of your brand will spring, including potential sub-brands in the future. It sets the tone for your organization or product. Once a name has been selected and implemented, it is an expensive and disruptive undertaking to go through the process of changing that name, which is why it is so important to get it right the first time.

To find the perfect brand name for your product or company, you can either hire a professional or try the do-it-yourself method. With the right blend of talent, creativity, and perseverance, you may be able to come up with that clever name you've been seeking. However, what might seem like an easy task at the outset can quickly become incredibly challenging. Constraints such as finding a unique name with an available .com domain that can be trademarked will limit choices and force you to expand your imagination— possibly beyond your time and creative capabilities. Hiring a professional can help ensure that you end up with a great name and the peace of mind that it will be with you for the lifetime of your brand.

CHARACTERISTICS OF A GREAT NAME

When selecting the best name for your company or product, you should look for certain characteristics:

Short and Easy to Pronounce

Aim for a name with three syllables or less. Test the pronunciation of your name by pretending to answer the phone—how does it sound and feel? Is it easy to say, and does it sound established and trustworthy?

Meets Your Needs Online

Many of the top brands in the world own their domain names outright. While this is an ideal vision, your brand's flexibility with .com ownership depends on the type of business you are creating and how heavily you will rely on your website. See page 61 for further guidance on choosing a domain name that is right for you. Rule of thumb: If you want to launch as a brand, you should own the .com domain in order to "walk the walk."

Passes the Search Test

Do a Google search on your desired name to make sure it doesn't appear in similar or related products. Reviewing results of the first two or three pages should be sufficient to help you catch any red flags; your new brand will quickly infiltrate the first pages on Google anyway. This test will also help you weed out names that are already legally trademarked. Refer to page 66 for more information on trademarking your company name.

Tells a Story

When people ask you what your company or product name means (and they will), make sure it comes with a good story to back it up. There is so much competition in the marketplace, and consumers are seeking more than just a product—they are seeking to connect with your brand on an emotional level. The story behind your name can become a large part of that connection.

Stands Out (but Not Too Far) from Your Competitors' Product or Company Names

Selecting a name that allows you to stand out from other companies and products in your vertical will allow you to gain your consumers' attention. Be careful, though, not to choose a name so distinctively different that it no longer feels associated with your industry, or you'll run the risk that your target audience won't be able to quickly connect with it.

Expandable into Brand Language

Think of Twitter and how it has made clever use of its name by creating a whole culture with its very own nomenclature—comments are dubbed "tweets" and the world of Twitter is known as the "Twittersphere." This aspect of a name may not be applicable to your specific product or company launch, but it can be a nice bonus and may be able to evolve organically over time.

Avoids Clichés or Overused Words

Within your particular industry or vertical, there are likely a number of words that many companies have used in their names. For example, if you're launching a new line of cosmetics, you would be wise to avoid using the word (or any derivation of the word) "beauty" in your product line. This overused term has become passé over time. Using a clichéd word can make your product feel dated before it even hits the shelves, also making it more difficult to be found via online searches.

Culturally Friendly

A key factor for brands that will reach a global audience (and most brands will through their various social media outlets) is that the brand name should resonate across cultures. Make sure you've researched the breadth of meanings and connotations your chosen name might carry.

> **> FURTHER READING**
>
> Launch Glocally – Not A Choice, But A Necessity
> *tinyurl.com/launchglocally*

TYPES OF BRAND NAMES

Now that you are well versed in the ingredients involved in selecting a great company name, let's take a look at the various types of names available. In her book *Designing Brand Identity*, author Alina Wheeler identifies six major categories for types of brand names: founder, descriptive, fabricated, metaphor, acronym, and creative spelling (Wheeler, 2013). Adding to this list, we've included a category for numeric names as well. Below, we will explore each of these categories further and weigh the pros and cons of each of these types of brand names.

Founder

Companies or products named for their founders tend to lean toward the more conservative side. Examples include Johnson & Johnson and the Bill & Melinda Gates Foundation.

+ **Pros:** Recognition or legacy associated with the name can allow your brand to have an instant following among those already familiar with the founder. It will likely be quite easy to obtain a trademark on a brand name based on its founder. The chances of another brand in your industry having the same name are slim, unless, of course, the founder name is very common, such as "John Smith."

- **Cons:** As in the case of Martha Stewart and Lance Armstrong, when a product or company is linked to a well-known name, any press that follows that person will follow your brand. Be sure you are ready to weather any storm with a fearless PR agency in tow, and having an exit strategy in place for if the founder leaves the namesake company.

Descriptive

As the category implies, some brand names evoke precisely what they do, as in the case of Match.com, Kickstarter, YouTube, and Petco.

+ **Pros:** This type of name quickly conveys your purpose to your consumer, which can translate to fewer marketing dollars spent on educating your target audience.

- **Cons:** With the quickly diminishing list of available .com domain names, finding a descriptive name for your company can be especially challenging. Additionally, there may be numerous other companies within your vertical that have either the same or a very similar name, which can make it very difficult to trademark and stand out. Relying on a specific feature of your company too much for your name poses a threat as your startup's core offerings change over time. An example mentioned earlier, the company YouSendIt faced this exact dilemma when they had to rename their company to Hightail because they had expanded their product line to offer more than just file sending.

> "They say peculiar names, by themselves, may mean nothing to begin with. But if backed by a successful branding campaign, they will come to signify whatever the companies want them to mean."
>
> — *from thought piece on Knowledge@Wharton blog, University of Pennsylvania*

Fabricated

These names consist of a made-up word or a combination of words that create something new. Examples include Accenture, which was derived from "Accent on the Future" and Xobni, which is "inbox" spelled backwards.

+ **Pros:** Fabricated names can lead to some of the strongest branding for a product or company. Consider Kleenex and Xerox: both names have become synonymous with their products. This type of names can be the easiest to trademark simply because they tend to be unique.

- **Cons:** A fabricated name is unlikely to communicate immediately to the consumer what your company or product is about. It will require a larger marketing effort and budget to educate your target audience.

Metaphor

These names describe the nature of a company through reference to people, places, things, or foreign words. Puma, a popular brand of athletic wear, uses the metaphor of a fast, agile animal to communicate its brand.

+ **Pros:** Metaphorical names can serve as a creative way to convey your brand without being overly obvious. They help you avoid those clichés and overused terms discussed earlier in the "Characteristics of a Great Name" section.

- **Cons:** Misleading connotations can cause confusion and allow your brand to slip into oblivion unless you have the correct marketing effort to educate your audience; these can also be more difficult to find in online searches. Names that reference common words can be quite difficult to trademark because there may be many other products or companies within your industry that have already used that term in the naming of their brand.

Acronym

These names form a new word or words based on acronyms that carry a message relatable to the new brand. AOL is derived from "America On-Line" and Asics is an acronym for "anima sana in corpore sano," which, translated from Latin, means "healthy soul in a healthy body."

+ **Pros:** With names that cannot be read as a word, such as AOL, shorter acronym names can allow your company to quickly sound like a well-established large brand. Similar to descriptive company names, if your acronym spells out a unique name, as in the example of Asics, obtaining a trademark shouldn't be problematic.

- **Cons:** Depending on the length of the acronym, it can be very difficult to obtain an available .com domain, particularly in the case of three- or four-letter names. In addition, you will need to expend additional marketing effort to ensure that your audience won't jumble or confuse the letters of your brand name.

Creative Spelling

These names alter the spelling of a relatively common word, as exemplified in the names of brands such as Svpply, a product aggregation site, and Lyft, a ride-sharing service. Names such as Svpply and Lyft tend to appeal to a younger demographic.

+ Pros: It can be an easy way to obtain a domain with the name you want.

- Cons: Consumers will likely misspell your company name in web searches if they've heard it only mentioned verbally. Or they may be unsure as how to pronounce it if they've only seen it written, and therefore might be less inclined to repeat it to a friend. Even if other brands in your vertical spell their name somewhat differently, you might have a hard time obtaining a trademark on this type of name if the United States Patent and Trademark Office (USPTO) deems that it can cause confusion. This naming strategy can often be seen as lazy.

THE NAME-LETTER BRANDING PHENOMENON

Did you know that your name can have an impact on everything from your day-to-day decisions (such as which candy bar to buy) to some of your most important life decisions (such as the career you choose)?

"If a brand name shares our initials, we tend to like it more" (Bonezzi, 2009), says Miguel Brendl, professor of marketing at the Kellogg School of Management, who has taken an interest in studying the people's complex relationships with their names and the brands they purchase. It is no coincidence that there are an unusual number of dentists named Dennis. Women named Louise are likely to move to Louisiana, and Craigs like Coke while Peters prefer Pepsi. Is it any coincidence then, that my name, being the principal of FINIEN, is Fabian? I think not.

Numeric

This category comprises names that consist only of a number or that combine a word with a number to convey a unique story about their brand. For example, the household cleaner Formula 409 (more commonly referred to as just "409") got its name through perseverance.

> **FURTHER READING**

How To Win The Numbers Game With Your Brand Name

tinyurl.com/winnumbersgame

After creating and testing 408 different formula versions, two young scientists in Detroit developed the winning blend we use today (source: formula409.com).

+ **Pros:** Creating a story between a word and a number can make for a memorable name. Combining a common word with a number that tells a distinct story about your company or product can also make it easier to secure a domain and trademark.

− **Cons:** It might be difficult to secure a domain if the name only has 3–4 numbers. Longer numeric names can be difficult for your audience to remember.

SELECTING THE FINAL NAME

After numerous brainstorming sessions, you will likely have a list of about 40–100 name options for your new brand. In an ideal situation, your options will be so great that it will be difficult to narrow them down to just one selection. Here are some rules of thumb to help guide your final decision-making process:

Make sure it meets your initial criteria.

Refer back to the list "Characteristics of a Great Name." Which of those items stood out to you as being most important for your new brand? Now take a look at your list of potential names and decide which of these names fulfills most of the criteria you were seeking from the start.

Sell your team.

So you feel like you've found the right name for your company moving forward. If that's the case, don't open it up for the emotional, unproductive feedback typical of a larger group. If you ask your significant other, she or he will likely react emotionally and might not understand the full strategy, research, and context. She or he will hear an unfamiliar name and will immediately sense danger. If you ask your coworkers, they might have similar feelings and fears about their professional future within your company: "What if the name backfires? Why does our fearless leader have to ask us? Is it not a good name?"

They should be afraid. Naming is a scary thing, but luckily for them, you already did that part and you're confident that you're on the right path. That said, sometimes you just have to ask to give yourself peace of mind and to provide your key partners with a feeling of ownership prior to officially taking this significant step.

Present a clear case as to why a name change is necessary, tell them that you've narrowed it down to one or two final names after hiring a professional naming agency (if applicable), and say that you have a clear favorite and explain why. You now want their buy-in (what you will get is their opinion) just in case you forgot anything when making that decision (and to make sure they're "in the know" for the big announcement). If you're about to have that meeting, here's how to go about it the right way:

1. **Define the confidants; they will define the outcome.** Who should be the two to four people whom you want to gain feedback or buy-in from? Choose them based on their involvement in your company. They may be cofounders or partners, but they shouldn't be freelancers or non–VC-level employees or peers. This is not intended to discriminate, but to keep it to a very small and influential group that you'd like to support you during the rollout phase.

2. **Be confident. Be assured.** Tell them you have made up your mind, even if you're still split between two names. Explain why the change was necessary. Share how long the process took and how many names you went through to get there. If applicable, share that they've been professionally derived and vetted and that you feel very excited about the new company/product

name. It's a new era, and you're thrilled to let them in early on.

3. Story first. Names later. Present them with only one or two names. Even if you're still indecisive, sound assertive. If your presentation feels insecure, they will sense it and feed that fire. First, tell the story behind each name as well as the meaning and the keywords that have been used—only then is it recommended to reveal the name to them. After sharing the backstory, say the name out loud while showing it on screen or on paper. As they familiarize themselves with the name, tell them your grand vision for how clients and coworkers will use it, how it sounds when answering the phone, how great it will look visually, and how the name really tells the story of your company without limiting your future growth. Repeat this process for option two, all while keeping the next rule in mind.

4. Leave the past behind: Say hello to the future. While looking at the new naming options, most will associate only with the past (Henry Ford's quote comes to mind: "If I had asked people what they wanted, they would have said faster horses."). You'll have to reiterate the idea that this new word soon will represent not any current connotations, but instead your company. Your mind-set is already focused on the future; if you're renaming, you are already emotionally detached from the current name and attached to the new name. It will be a big challenge for them to overcome. Remember our name, FINIEN? The (short and rather brilliant) name would have likely died by committee based on past associations. Today, you hear FINIEN and you think about branding, startups, this book you have read, and perhaps me. It's how it works. Brands are being built. You have to explain why it's necessary to think of the name six months from today. Try not to associate any words with the name, but rather the image of your company.

Gaining buy-in is crucial to finding a great name. Use these points to prep for the meeting that may decide the future of your brand's name. And, most important, trust your gut.

The following chart breaks down the reasons why we chose our consultancy's name, FINIEN:

01 SIGNIFICANCE

Latin: 'finiens'= compass
Polynesian: 'finien' = seed
French: 'finir' = completed

02 LINGUISTIC CLARITY

pronunciation: fin-ee-en
simplicity: 6 letters
tonality: energetic, bold

03 DISTINCTION

uniqueness: stands out
memorability: repetition in sound
visual recognition: angular letters

04 MARKETABILITY

web availability: finien.com
trademarkable: brand protection

CHOOSING A DOMAIN

Naming your brand successfully and formulating your domain name go hand in hand. Every startup has different needs when it comes to domain ownership. Is owning your .com domain outright the only way to go? Or are there other ways you can have success with a creatively modified domain? Even if you have already answered these questions, factors such as domain availability, pricing, and trademark rights will all influence your final decision. With the following graphics, we offer a personalized guide to help you make strategic and informed decisions as you go through the process of choosing your new domain name.

You search for the .com domain name you want on a domain registration website. What are your results?

Available

Does your name meet the following criteria?

- memorable
- succinct
- easily spelled
- doesn't infringe on trademarks
- matches your brand

No   Yes

Reconsider if this is the right name for your domain. Not meeting the aforementionted criteria could lead to confusion for your audience when they try to find you online. Your domain name is a branding tool that should reinforce the recognizability and distinction of your brand.

Up for Auction

Are you willing to bid for the domain?

Yes   No

Choose a new domain name or try a modified version of the domain you want. Visit page 65 for alternative options.

If your desired domain name is up for grabs, register it as soon as possible. Most domain hosting services charge a $10-15 fee to keep a domain registered each year. This a very small investment considering the tremendous value a .com domain will bring to your new brand. If your domain is at auction, the price will depend on what other interested buyers are willing to pay. In order to figure out how much it is worth to you, see page 65.

Not Available

Are you able and willing to contact and purchase it from the existing owner?

No   Yes

See next page

Purchasing a domain name from an existing owner

Is the .com owned and maintained by a currently operating business?

Yes   No

Even if the existing owner is open to selling the domain, it is better to have a domain that is unique to your business than one that could easily be confused with another brand. See page 65 for plan B strategies you can use to make your domain name work for you.

Is the owner willing to sell the domain?

Yes   No

Choose a new domain name or try a modified version of the domain you want. See page 65 for alternative options.

Are you willing to pay the asking price or to negotiate?

Yes   No

Most owners who are sitting on an unused domain name are willing to negotiate a fair price based on the desirability of the name and your needs. For help figuring out how much the domain is worth to you, see page 65.

If the owner is open to selling the domain, but is asking for much more than you are ready or able to offer at this stage of your startup, conduct some research (see page 65) to help you negotiate. If that does not work, choose a new domain name or try a modified version of the domain you want. See page 65 for guidance.

**What to do when the .com domain name
for you brand is unavailable**

Is your product or
service first and
foremost an online
destination? (think
Amazon and Reddit)

Yes   No

Owning the .com is a
top priority for your
brand. If you know
your audience will
always associate
your domain name
with your service
or product, having
the .com will add
tremendous value
to your brand.
Go back to your
naming process
and only consider
names that you can
register. You are
more likely to have
success with names
that are either
fabricated, numeric,
or creatively spelled,
although each of
these types of names
have their benefits
and drawbacks.

Would you consider
incorporating a
qualifier or using a
different Top Level
Domain (TLD) such
as .co or .net?

No   Yes

If you are flexible
with the structure of
your domain name,
you will have much
better odds of finding
an available domain
using a qualifier
or alternative TLD.
Please see page 65
for guidance.

How much money is a .com domain worth?

Most startups can expect to pay at least $500 to $5,000 for a quality .com domain name; however, pricing a domain is not an exact science and can go into six and seven digits. Fund.com sold for $9,999,950 and slots.com for $5,500,000. As in buying real estate offline, many factors affect the price of a domain. According to the domain experts at DN Sale Price (an online database tracking the sales history of domain names) these factors include length, number of words, spelling, commercial potential, brandability, memorability, search engine potential, and more. To get a better sense of what your domain is worth, start by reviewing the history of domain sales with similar structures or keywords on websites such as DNSalePrice.com or NameBio.com.

Alternatives to "brand.com" ownership

While owning a .com is the most desirable way to go, your brand can still have success with a carefully chosen top-level domain (TLD). If you decide to go this route, make sure the owners of the .com are not in the same industry, as this can lead to customer confusion, brand dilution, and trademarking disputes. Below are some recommended alternative options:

- **.net** – This is the second most popular extension after .com. It was originally intended for network use but is open to anyone; it has established itself as a respectable, though slightly dated, alternative to .com.

- **.org** – This TLD is often associated with nonprofits, open-source content, and cause-related websites, but anyone can register with this extension.

- **.co** – Popular among tech innovators, entrepreneurs, and startups, including AngelList (angel.co) and VINE (vine.co). It was originally a country extension for Colombia but is now open for general registration.

- **.pro/.shoes/.bike etc.** – A number of industry-specific extensions have started to gain popularity. They are pricier to register, but if your brand falls into one of the offered categories, a unique extension can be a good solution. A caveat, though: customer adaptation rates are still an unknown. For a current list of extensions and their restrictions, visit *tinyurl.com/tldextensions*.

Come up with a list of qualifiers that you believe work with your domain (without diluting your brand) to help you get around a .com that is taken. Let's say you are launching a new educational product for kids and you want to name it "BrainWhiz," but the .com domain name is taken. You may consider adding "kids" to buy the domain "BrainWhizKids.com."

If you are launching a landing page for an app that will be found mainly in app stores on mobile devices, a structure such as get_(app name)_.com or _(app name)app.com is a great way to own your .com and set apart your app from other products with similar names.

Another way to think about descriptors is through the lens of your brand purpose and personality. For example, the brand Bolla is a Los Angeles-based company offering goods that relate to skateboarding, art, design, and pop/street culture. The artist who started the brand states, "My life motto is Carpe Diem. Pretty much put in everything you got or nothing, go hard or go home. Kill at everything I do" (James H. Yukawa). His brand embodies this spirit and is reflected in his domain choice, BollaKills.com, which caters to the young urban community. Another example of a creative domain solution comes from the mobile meditation app Headspace. The app was created to help people get more "headspace" through a regular guided meditation practice, so they appropriately named their website getsomeheadspace.com.

TRADEMARKS

Once you've chosen the name for your new brand, it's time to check the IP rights so that you can make it official. Trademarking the name ensures that you own it and won't encounter any issues down the road from another company claiming to have the same or a similar name. It also protects you from those who might try to copy or illegally acquire your name.

If you haven't already done so, begin your trademark search by running the name through a search engine such as Google, as recommended earlier under "Characteristics of a Great Name: Passes the Search Test." Once your name passes the search test with flying colors, visit the United States Patent and Trademark Office website (www.uspto.gov). Using its search tool, TESS, run a basic search to see if any other trademarks under your desired company name appear. If a similar name within the same industry appears in your search results, your trademark approval will likely get denied. If no similar results appear, it's time to move on to the next step of filing for a trademark. If you're seeking a swift trademark process, launch your website before filing for a trademark. Understand that you are taking on the risk of not obtaining the mark in the end, but launching your website will mean less required paperwork and possibly less time to obtain an approval, especially if you have a product already on the market under your brand's name. If time is not of the essence and you wish to lower your risk factor, file for the trademark before moving on to the process of creating the brand identity and designing the website. The two most popular options for filing are contracting with a trademark attorney or choosing a service such as LegalZoom (US) to help guide you through the process.

NAMING:
Takeaways & Insights

+ Most startups change their core business
  model as they grow, especially in the first
  6–12 months after launch. In the case of an
  ill-advised naming strategy, the name also
  has to change.

+ Ideas, processes, offerings, designs, and
  teams will all likely adapt over time, but your
  name will stay with you forever.

+ Ensure that you own the rights to your
  chosen brand name: purchase the domain,
  get the social media channels, and
  trademark the name.

+ Ensure that the name already tells a story or
  can be easily used to create a new story.

IDENTITY DESIGN

Be mindful of how your brand mark reflects the core principles of your Brand Platform. Your design doesn't have to capture the entire story of your brand, but it should represent a unified idea about the purpose of your brand.

Font: Futura

03: IDENTITY DESIGN

Brand identity starts with a simplified mark that identifies your brand through a symbol, wordmark, or letterform mark. It is one of the most important pieces of your branding because it creates an immediate visual and emotional connection with your audience. An agency or designer that provides quality identity design services should use an in-depth process that explores various concepts and visual solutions. Your design partner should also keep in mind that your brand mark will eventually be incorporated into a larger identity system for your brand.

Dharma Singh Khalsa, MD, asserts that the average American sees 16,000 logos, advertisements, and labels in a single day (Airey, 2010). In the book *Logo Design Love*, author David Airey challenges readers to take a quick glance around their immediate surroundings. If you do this, chances are you can spot at least ten logos—unless, of course, you are reading this from the top of Mount Everest. Even there, a quick glance down at your clothing and gear could easily yield a fair number of logos. With this overload of information, it's more important than ever to create a unique identity that will stand out in the crowd.

Selecting one simple, distinctive, and memorable mark that will communicate your company to the public may seem like a daunting task, but the considerable effort you've already put into your Brand Platform means that you're halfway there. Look back at the adjectives you listed that would describe your brand's personality in chapter 1, "Brand Platform," on page 37. These should be the key terms your creative team uses as the basis for the design direction.

FORMS OF IDENTITY DESIGN

Of the 16,000 logos you see on any given day, each falls into one of two categories that comprise the basic types of identity design:

Wordmark: This style of identity design is one in which the company name stands alone to represent the brand. Typography is of utmost importance. Choosing and customizing or creating a distinctive typeface will be the key differentiator for your brand. Truly clever wordmark designs may also contain hidden symbols. Take the FedEx logo, for example. The white space between the letters "e" and "x" reveals a forward-pointing arrow, indicating speed and movement—two very important attributes of the overall brand. If you've never noticed this element before, we guarantee you it will be the first thing you see when you look at this wordmark from now on.

Icon and wordmark: This style pairs a wordmark with a symbol or shape. Ideally, the symbol or shape will become so recognizable for your brand over time that it can eventually stand alone as your identity design. Think of how iconic the symbols for both Nike and Target have become. Even though we don't show you the logos here in the book, you are able to picture them in your mind and associate them with the brands. The basic icon categories are defined as the following:

Abstract symbols: Symbols that are invented and inherently have no meaning. The brand must build the meaning around the symbol (Adams, Morioka, and Stone, 2004)

Metaphoric: Recognizable shapes or images that convey the brand values, services, or attributes (Adams, Morioka, and Stone, 2004)

Literal: An icon or symbol that is an obvious representation of the brand itself

Pictorial: Detailed imagery that tells a story about the brand

SEVEN COMPONENTS TO LOOK FOR IN A GREAT IDENTITY DESIGN

Timeless

A timeless brand identity mark will represent your company conceptually and visually for the life of your brand. Consider the Coca-Cola brand. It has one of the most recognizable and timeless identities on the market with its custom scripted logotype. The brand identity blog Under Consideration has documented the transformation of the Coca-Cola and Pepsi identities between 1940 and now (source: http://tinyurl.com/colavspepsi). Both beverages have explored various lock-ups over the years. A comparison timeline reveals that while Pepsi has undergone dramatic logotype style changes, the basic scripted Coca-Cola logotype has retained the same character.

Though you want your original brand mark to stay relevant as long as possible, it is acceptable to let it evolve naturally as your brand reaches key turning points or milestones over the course of a few decades. Your initial brand mark is still a critical part of your brand foundation and should be strong enough to lend itself to evolution without requiring a conceptual revolution.

Starbucks has gone through the identity evolution process gracefully over the course of forty years. Its three redesigns have demonstrated the strength of the Starbucks brand identity. Starbucks has gradually simplified its iconic core illustration (the mermaid in a green circle) without compromising recognizability. In 2011, Starbucks completely removed the logotype from its primary identity mark, which only a very few brands—among them Nike with its famous swoosh—have achieved successfully.

Coca-Cola is the quintessential timeless brand, but many entrepreneurs have a tough time replicating its success because they're drawn to the latest fads. Unfortunately, that's not the key ingredient for enduring the test of time. If it's a current trend, it's unlikely to be one in the future. Most trends don't hold up over time. A trend is cool for a very short time, then quickly turns into an annoyance. The more honest and creative you are when crafting your brand identity, the more likely it is that you'll create something timeless.

"If you can't explain the
idea (behind the logo)
in one sentence over the
telephone, it won't work"

— *Lou Danziger, as quoted in*
Logo Design Workbook (Adams,
Morioka, & Stone, 2004)

Your logo can still be modern, exciting, and speak to a young audience—it just cannot look like a trend. How would you know? Your idea might have been derived from something you saw, maybe you liked it because it looked hip—maybe you've seen similar logos before and you felt yours should follow their lead. Don't. Lead rather than follow. First with your logo, then with the rest of your brand.

Unique/Distinct

Your brand mark is your quickest tool for distinguishing your brand from your competitors. Ensure that your agency carefully researches the identity design styles of your competitors before starting explorations. While you want your mark to make sense within your industry, you do not want to confuse your audience or encroach on the identity of a competitor. Your design should offer a unique perspective that only your brand can claim.

Dive deep into your own beliefs. Nail down what you're about as a company based on your core values, then determine how you want to communicate that to your target audience. Once you decide exactly what message you want to get across to your audience, you can create a truly unique visual and verbal brand language that will stand the test of time.

Tells a story

Your design doesn't have to capture the entire story of your brand, but it should represent a unified idea about the purpose of your brand. Every design decision that shapes your brand mark will contribute to this narrative, which can be represented through shapes, symbols, styles, colors, and typography.

Take Amazon as an example. The Amazon.com logo looks deceptively simple at first glance, but if you contemplate the placement of the arrow below the logotype you will see it is communicating something deeper about the experience Amazon aims to give its customers. The arrow points from the a to the z, which alludes to the wide range of products that the site sells. Moreover, the shape of the arrow forms a reassuring grin.

Simple

When you review an identity design, consider what it will look like if it is condensed down to only its most essential components. Any additional elements that are unnecessary for communication could add clutter and distract from your brand message. A good design can say a lot without overwhelming its audience.

Flexible

Allow for variations in the application of the identity design across print and media. Your logo may live in different lock-ups as an identity mark only or a logotype only. A brand mark should also work effectively in black-and-white formats when color production is not an option. Technically limiting applications, such as on-garment embroidery, may surface during the life of your brand. If your identity is designed in a flexible way, it can weather those storms gracefully.

Works Well as Both Large and Small Sizes

Keep in mind how your brand mark will be reproduced across various media. When it is resized for a business card or Twitter icon, does it retain readability and recognizability? In addition, always ensure that your agency builds your design in vector format. This enables you to resize your

> **> FURTHER READING**
>
> Infographic: Your New Brand In Pixels – 6 Ways To Scale Your Brand's Identity
> *tinyurl.com/brandinpixels*

logo freely without worrying about degrading the quality of your design. In some instances, your design firm might create slight logo variations for different size usages, which is a way to ensure maximum readability.

Adaptive (on a Case-by-Case Basis to be Determined at the Outset of a Project)

Depending on the architecture of your brand, you may need to think about designing a system of sub-identities that lock up with your brandmark or logotype. Some brands, such as FedEx, function as umbrellas for various lines of business (see "Establishing Your Brand Architecture" on page 40) and need an adaptive identity system to unify the brand. FedEx does this by using color distinctions. While all of its sub-brand marks share a unifying logotype design and a purple "Fed," the color of the "Ex" is different for each line of business: FedEx Freight uses red, FedEx Express is orange, FedEx Ground uses green, and so on.

LEVERAGING THE THREE CORE COMPONENTS OF YOUR BRAND IDENTITY TO ENHANCE MESSAGING

When most people think about the word brand they first think of logo (even though you now know a brand is much more than its logo). The logo is the key point of visual interaction with a brand, and we are likely to recall it every time we think, talk, or write about a brand.

During the brand identity (logo) design process, entrepreneurs often forget that there are two other elements that help tell the company or product's story. These elements interact and bring value to the brand identity as a whole. Do not repeat the same message, but instead leverage these three core components to create a stronger, deeper brand message:

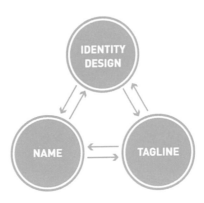

If your name describes your business, do not focus on showing the same message in your logo; instead use your logo to talk about other key elements that describe and differentiate your business. If you are in the cloud storage business and your name includes the two words cloud and storage (a bad company name, yet a good example is 'Cloud Storage Ninjas'), have your logo visualize security and stability, if those are key components of your brand's message. To the contrary, if your name is nondescript, either fabricated or an acronym, ensure that the associated brand identity design visualizes what you are in business for (e.g., cloud storage).

Often forgotten during and beyond the brand identity design process is the *tagline*. There are many factors to blame for the slow ongoing extinction of the tagline (mainly of a digital nature, as taglines are hard to squeeze into apps and templated websites), but the power of a great tagline is still immense (Just do it, we say!). The tagline should be alive and kicking even though its placement has changed from its traditional location below the brand identity design. It can now be used as the first header visitors see on a brand's website or the descriptor below the company name in an e-mail signature, it can replace yet another step-and-repeat icon pattern on a back of a business card, or it can be used in the often underestimated— yet early—brand touch point, the lobby of a business. The tagline is a powerful tool that, together with the name and brand identity design, tells a stronger, deeper, and more actionable initial brand story. It is the leading actor, and you can write the script.

TRADEMARKING YOUR BRAND IDENTITY MARK

In addition to your name, make sure you register a trademark for your identity design, even if it is a logotype of a name that has already been trademarked. The process of trademarking a design is similar to that of trademarking a name or any other brand element, but the USPTO search process is more complex. Each distinct design element in your mark will need to be interpreted, coded, and searched. The USPTO website provides a coded table of design categories for reference. For small companies that want assistance with this process, LegalZoom offers a service that files your trademark application to the USPTO and performs a basic search for you.

IDENTITY DESIGN:
Takeaways & Insights

+ Don't rush into the Identity Design Phase.

+ Particularly if you are a startup in the tech space, ensure that you have sufficiently prototyped your product or service before diving into this phase. It would be both inefficient and costly to design an identity that later needs to be revamped because the audience for the product/service has changed or the product/service itself has changed significantly.

+ Simplicity in design and depth in message are key to a successful identity design.

+ The simpler the logo, the more adaptable it will be, making it easier to create a strong Brand Atmosphere over time.

+ Your new logo shall not be hip; save trends for other marketing efforts, if necessary.

BRAND ATMOSPHERE
TOUCH POINTS

Each company has
unique needs in terms
of developing branded
elements for print, display,
digital, and environment.
Regardless of which
ones your strategy calls
for, remember that all
brands should focus on
how their Brand Platform
is integrated into each
touch point through
consistency in visual cues
and messaging.

Font: Frutiger

04: BRAND ATMOSPHERE TOUCH POINTS

Once you have established a solid platform, name, and identity design, you are ready to breathe life into your brand by expanding it through tangible materials and experiences. At FINIEN, we call these your Brand Atmosphere Touch Points. Each company has unique needs in terms of developing branded elements for print, display, digital, and environment. Regardless of which of these your strategy calls for, remember that all brands should focus on how their Brand Platform is consistently integrated into each touch point in visual cues and messaging. Seemingly small details in layout and design can have a huge impact on your brand's cohesiveness and success. "Design choices like color, layout, and font can compel the right audience to buy when they are used correctly—or repel your audience from buying when they are not," states Maria Ross, author of *Branding Basics* (2010, p. 58). Furthermore, these design choices will speak volumes about the values of your brand. "Visual expression often reveals the unspoken intentions behind corporate strategy" (*Minamiyama*, 2007, p. 29), confirm Uli Mayor-Johanssen (chief design officer, MetaDesign, AG) and Klaus-Peter Johanssen (managing partner, Johanssen + Kretschmer) in *World Branding*. How do your business cards, storefronts, and social media outlets harmonize to tell a larger story about your brand? In this chapter we will focus on creating your Brand Atmosphere while keeping these principles in mind.

SIGNIFICANCE OF COLOR

Color selection is a key part of your strategic Brand Atmosphere decision-making process that goes far beyond artistic preferences. Color influences an audience emotionally and is often the first thing people notice when they interact with a brand. If used correctly, it has the power to create positive associations and improve recognition with an audience. If misused, it can confuse or drive an audience away.

At this point in your process, you have likely worked with a creative partner who has chosen a color (or colors) for your identity design. This is often a good starting point for considering your brand's expanded color scheme. It is common for brands to have a primary color and one or two accent colors. Accent colors will open up a world of opportunity for integrating dynamic designs and functionality within your branding. We encourage all new brands to define a full color palette with their design firm before creating branded materials. Color consistency is critical for establishing a unified look and feel across all Brand Atmosphere Touch Points.

Choosing Your Color Palette

> **Color and Emotional Associations:** When you are presented with color options to implement throughout your Brand Atmosphere, consider how they represent your brand's personality. Each color comes with its own associations. For example, orange is associated with energy, playfulness, and boldness. Some iconic brands that use orange as their primary color are Nickelodeon, Home Depot, and Etsy. On the opposite end of the color wheel, blue evokes a sense of trust, calmness, and security. It is a popular color in corporate identity design. Chase Bank, Hewlett-Packard, General Electric, and Blue Shield are just a few major brands that leverage blue in their Brand Atmosphere.

> **Competition:** You will also want your design partners to research how your chosen colors compare to those of your brand's main competitors. Color can be an effective way of distinguishing your brand, as long as it makes sense in the context of your market and Brand Platform.

> **Readability:** Which colors are most suitable for foreground and background placement? For the sake of readability, most brands use

dark or bold colors in the foreground (especially for text) and light colors in the background. If you choose to go the opposite route, aim for high contrast between your foreground and background colors.

Color Theory: Consider how your colors relate to one another. Your accent colors should contrast your primary color to create visual interest. They can still share attributes such as brightness that allow them to work together in a layout. If you need help visualizing potential color palettes, the following websites provide inspiration and tools for creating balanced color combinations: kuler.adobe.com and colorschemedesigner.com.

CASE STUDY

Virgin America, recently acquired by Alaska Airlines, has successfully set itself apart from its domestic competitors in the past few years. One of its secrets to brand success is a bold approach to applying color. "For years, flying domestically had largely become a dismal, uninspired experience. When Virgin America launched, the idea that a domestic airline could reinvent that experience—through technology, design and entertainment—was still a pretty radical notion," said Luanne Calvert, VP of marketing at Virgin America, in a 2012 press release. The airline seeks to create an innovative, exciting, and luxurious flying experience, and those values are well represented in the bold red and deep purple hues it has chosen as part of its Brand Atmosphere. From the check-in counter to the airplane cabin, travelers interact regularly with Virgin America's distinctive colors, which are featured as accents on airplane tickets, luggage tags, digital entertainment systems, flight attendant uniforms, and of course the airplane graphics. Virgin America even uses purple mood lights in its cabin to evoke a classy nightclub atmosphere. Design Director Adam Wells explains, "It's in a 'theatrical mood' prior to departure, when you walk down the jet bridge, you see the purple glow of the mood lighting, and it hopefully excites you" (O'Neill, 2013).

COLOR IN DIFFERENT MEDIA

When color is reproduced, it will vary across various digital and print mediums. To ensure consistency, ask for Pantone standards (also known as spot colors) for each color in your palette and have them matched with CMYK (for print) and RGB (for digital) equivalents. Your chosen design team will help you identify which color profiles should be used for each project. However, it helps to understand the differences between the three basic color profiles:

CMYK (Cyan, Magenta, Yellow, Black): *Best option for digitally printed media. This process contains four percentage values for cyan, magenta, yellow, and black. For example, a pure yellow might be represented as C0 M0 Y100 K0.*

PMS (Pantone Matching System): *Universal color system for printing standards to maintain high quality on traditional printing presses. This is used for print jobs that require precise color matching, and because all of your brand's communications should look consistent, we recommend choosing Pantone colors to match CMYK jobs. It's as simple as telling the digital print vendor that the orange should be matched as closely as possible to Pantone 165C. Similar to paint samples, Pantone's color books allow customers to compare printed color options.*

RGB (Red, Green, Blue): *Used for digital display because each color combination is projected in the form of light rays. This model contains three color values from 0 to 255 for red, green, and blue. Yellow would read R225 G255 B0.*

SIGNIFICANCE OF TYPOGRAPHY

Typography is one of the most important design elements in your branded materials. When you consider typography options with your design team, keep readability and brand cohesion at the forefront of your mind. You want your chosen fonts to have attributes that support your brand identity without competing with your logotype font. Is your brand modern and casual? If so, you may want to see sans-serif font options. Is it built on tradition, or does it speak to an older demographic? A serif font might be better suited. You will also want to consider how your fonts communicate within different media (e.g., print, web) and at different sizes, weights, and colors. Not all fonts are available with both web and print licenses, so be sure to verify those details. Many times it will make sense to have more than one typeface in your branding materials—for example, a highly stylized font in headers and a simpler font for larger blocks of text. Reference the fundamental, easy-to-digest book Stop Stealing Sheep for further reading on this important subject. Resources for quality web/print fonts include FontFont.com, FontShop.com, Fonts.com, and MyFonts.com.

The chart below illustrates how FINIEN has organized brand colors, fonts, and graphic elements into primary and secondary themes for its client Martian Ranch & Vineyard:

	Color	Font	Brand Elements
Primary	PMS 7408	Mrs. Eaves	
Secondary	PMS 1807	STONE SANS	

The following examples demonstrate how FINIEN translated the design components from the previous chart into Brand Atmosphere Touch Points:

PHOTOGRAPHY CONSIDERATIONS

Planning your brand's photographic identity is another important aspect of your Brand Atmosphere. For most businesses this means choosing between purchasing stock photos online and hiring a professional photographer. Both options have their benefits and drawbacks, but on the whole, stock images are not a strong substitute for custom photography when establishing a new brand. Photography should enhance a brand's voice. Stock photos are often too generic and inconsistent in style to achieve this effectively. If you choose to use stock photos, you may want to have a design team add brand sensitivity to your photos to create a distinct photographic style. For example, you can apply a custom blur effect and a brand-colored duotone to all your stock images to create consistency. But your brand's unique point of view may not be inherent in stock photos, and this approach depends upon the involvement of designers manipulating your imagery. Custom photography requires a more significant investment of time and money overall, but the benefits of having a unique photographic expression will serve your brand in the long term.

Benefits of Custom Photography

No compromises: If you want an image of a strawberry cupcake reflected in a mirror and taken from a low angle with disco lighting in the background, you can make this happen. Relying on stock photography would probably require compromising on more than one of your criteria.

Originality and ownership: You can feel at ease knowing that the photos from your shoot are original and can be used without limitations and for your brand only. You will never have to worry about your competitor printing identical images in its brochures.

Brand customization: Your photographs can include elements unique to your brand, such as specific logos, products, locations, and people.

Artistic vision and consistent style: Hiring a professional gives you the benefit of lending his or her unique artistic perspective to your photos. For some brands, a particular photographer's vision even turns into the most recognizable part of their Brand Atmosphere.

Making the decision to hire a professional is a commitment, and you want to be sure it is a fruitful investment for your brand. Get the most out of this process by speaking with your photographer before the shoot to define what you want to achieve. We have created a set of questions to discuss with your team and photographer:

- *Where are your photos going to be used? (website, brochure, store, social media, etc.)*
- *What is the timeline for your photo shoot?*
- *What is your budget?*
- *How many shots do you need?*
- *What is the focus of your images? (people, products, locations, metaphors, etc.)*
- *If you are featuring people, do you need to hire models or gain consent from featured persons?*
- *Do you need to consider a wardrobe, props, makeup, and hair-styling?*
- *If you are featuring a specific location, do you need to rent a space or obtain a permit?*
- *Does your photographer have experience working with business and branding photography?*
- *What kind of story do you want to tell through your brand's imagery?*
- *How do you want your audience to relate or respond to your images?*
- *Is there a style that you want to run through all your photos?*

THE ART OF CRAFTING A BRAND VOICE

Tagline and descriptor

Establishing a strong tagline is the first step in developing your brand language. A tagline is a key phrase associated with your brand, and it is repeated across select marketing efforts and other elements of the Brand Atmosphere. Great taglines convey both the value and the essence of your brand in a concise and memorable way.

Before you work with a copywriter, review your brand's unique positioning outlined in the Brand Platform phase. It is important to define exactly what you are selling through your tagline. Developing one without a clear strategy can lead to confusion and can cause it to drift away from its original purpose. "We know storytelling will be the differentiator," says venture capitalist Tomasz Tungusz in an online thought piece on branding. "Kleenex manufactures tissues. But they sell an idea—'taking care of family'" (2013). Once you know what you want to say, your task is to mold that message into a catchy combination of words that will work seamlessly with your brand. Aim for a tagline that is five words or less.

> **FURTHER READING**

How Subliminal And Hidden Design Messages Can Boost Brand Engagement

tinyurl.com/subliminalbrand

At the outset of a new brand, you may first consider using a descriptor in place of a traditional tagline, primarily because it is important to fully understand what your brand is doing before you switch to a tagline that dives deeper into why you are doing it and what consumers can feel when using your product or service. For Nike, this may have been something along the lines of "Peak performance running shoes driven by design," and as the brand gained traction, it may have changed to the famous three words "Just do it." Our brand consultancy, FINIEN, nearly launched with "We know brands before they exist" but decided to clearly spell out what we are in business for instead: "Turning Ventures into Brands." If you choose that path, there is no need to get creative; just clearly spell out what your brand delivers to its user in the simplest way possible. If you choose to start out with a tagline, here are approaches to get you started:

Thought-provoking: Asks a question or makes someone pause to consider their relationship with the brand.

Example: "Are you in good hands?" —Allstate

Descriptive: Describes a quality of the product or service you are selling.

Example: "A diamond is forever." —DeBeers

Motivational: Inspires people to take action or aspire to a certain way of living.

Examples: "Just do it." —Nike, "Share moments. Share life" —Kodak

Comparative: Elevates the brand to a superior rank among its competitors.

Example: "The ultimate driving machine." —BMW

Voice

What you say and how you say things shape the perception of your brand. A carefully honed brand voice can establish credibility in your organization. Another way to consider voice is to refer back to the type of person you identified as an embodiment of your brand personality. What are this person's favorite phrases? How does your person interact with others? What kinds of stories does this person like to tell? Come up with a few key words to describe your brand voice as you consider the following four dimensions of brand voice originally identified by social media marketing expert Stephanie Schwab:

> **Tone:** *Tone* refers to an intrinsic quality of relating that comes across in your communications. Does your brand take a personal and humble approach to communicating, or is it more scientific and direct?
>
> **Character/Persona:** If you want your brand to be regarded as the ultimate standard or expert in your field, you may take on an authoritative and scholarly persona. A brand that sells outdoor gear may manifest a persona that is adventurous and eco-conscious.
>
> **Language:** Choose words and phrases that support the tone and persona your brand embodies. A brand designed to come across as serious and exclusive may choose to include industry-specific jargon in its communication. A brand meant to entertain may employ humor and use more casual language. As a general rule, you want the words that you incorporate to create positive associations with your brand. Also consider how you can create a language around your brand with phrases that you can take ownership of. Custom names for specific processes, services, products, and places will strengthen your brand voice.
>
> **Purpose:** Before you begin communicating, determine who you are

speaking with and why you are communicating in the first place. Are you primarily interested in spreading awareness about a cause and garnering support? Or are you hoping to get people to buy your products? Your purpose will inform the content you choose to focus on.

CASE STUDY

"There's one brand," writes *Brand Sense* author Martin Lindstrom, "that has scored higher in purloining language than any other. It is a brand that welcomes you to its kingdom of fantasy, dreams, promises, and magic" (2011, p. 50). Can you guess which brand Lindstrom is referring to? Anyone familiar with Disney—whether through the web, television, movies, parks and resorts, or radio—has been lulled by the enchanting language of "Disneyspeak." Through consistent promotion of the ideals of magic, dreams, and fantasy, Disney has seeded strong associations in our minds with seemingly generic words. Beyond adopting associations, Disney has coined exclusive brand vocabulary such as *Fastpass*, *Parkhopper*, and *Imagineer*. The brand further engrains its values by establishing language policies at its parks and stores. Disney employees are allowed to refer to their customers only as "guests" and to their fellow employees as "cast members."

THE POWER OF SOCIAL MEDIA BRANDING

Social media provides a huge opportunity for brands to grow their influence in a cost-efficient manner. In recent years, social media platforms have created a bustling online hub for interaction between people and businesses.

How you leverage your brand through social media channels will have a significant impact on your brand's success, especially if your business relies on online engagement, which is most frequently the case. Even retail brands "presell" products via online engagement. Purchasing-decision processes often occur online, even if the physical purchase happens elsewhere. For all brands, one thing holds true: customer relationships, PR, and service all take place via social media channels regardless of whether the brands are actively involved. Before you (or the social media agency you hire) dive into social media, we recommend that you develop a solid content strategy. Here are a few items to consider along the way:

Content value

Social media is a great space for direct marketing, but you need to provide value to your followers with useful content. Your brand will stay more relevant in your audience's minds if you add something valuable to their day. Although your audience may be interested in hearing about your latest product offerings and benefits, they are also interested in other aspects of your business in order to connect with your brand on a deeper level. You can share what goes on behind the scenes, interesting articles, or tidbits of advice. Make sure you understand your customers so that you can tailor your content for their lifestyles and interests and communicate directly with the your target market.

Brand voice

Social media is one of the most important channels for showcasing your unique brand voice. Refer back to the four dimensions of brand voice on page 95 for guidelines.

Maintenance and resources

Consider how much budget, staff, and time your business can dedicate to social media. Expect to spend a minimum of three to four hours per week to maintain a few basic accounts. It is better to have one or two well-maintained accounts than a handful of sparsely populated ones. If you choose to set up many, create a plan for allocating resources ahead of time or plan to keep some parked without content or advertising. Don't fall for every new hip social media platform (hundreds emerge at any given moment). Analyze them and find the ones that bring value to both your brand and your customers. Only commit to a new platform if you can dedicate time to populate it regularly.

Social Media Prelaunch Considerations

Secure branded domain names and usernames for all applicable sites. If your desired name is not available, consider adding an appropriate descriptor. For example, if you are branding a new cafe called Ceylon, you can try Ceylon_Cafe or Ceylon_SantaMonica. Because this can hurt your brand in some channels, we strongly advise creating brand names that are unique in the naming phase (see page 53), ensuring that domain names and social media handles can be secured more easily.

UI/UX DESIGN

No brand launch is complete without a solid digital strategy. Your online presence will serve as your primary brand communication tool. Bear in mind that your digital strategy will likely evolve many times over the years as technology and user behaviors change. It is important to stay up to date on current technologies, trends, and best practices to ensure that your online presence continuously supplements your brand in a successful way.

There are multiple phases involved in developing and implementing your digital strategy, and each one is as important as the next. If you haven't already done so, it's imperative that you gather a team of professionals for this important brand launch task.

As technologies and approaches change frequently, we have excluded the website discovery and planning, information architecture, design, and development steps from this book and instead offer an up-to-date white paper on this subject. Download it at http://tinyurl.com/ FourPhases.

Use custom designs for header areas, profile icons, and backgrounds to unify your brand image across social media platforms. Update all channels as you change your main website look, or be campaign-specific in channels when appropriate.

Decide how your website and other brand collateral will integrate social media links and feeds. There are many opportunities besides simply placing social media icons in the footer of your site—such as making quotes "tweetable" and "liking" certain parts of content. Because content creation is time-intensive, be sure to allow your users to share easily and transform your content from static to viral by asking questions or integrating user polls.

Start planning and writing posts in advance of your brand launch. Posting early can help you gain momentum faster once you go live. Potential followers will already see the valuable content you provide, and that will give them a reason to follow you. Early posting also allows the person in charge of the content creation to gain experience prior to having a "live" audience.

ENVISIONING THE BRAND ENVIRONMENT

Environment influences the mood and feelings that people associate with your brand. Elements that create a physical brand environment involve all of the five senses and can include architecture, materials, light, smell, and temperature. With environmental design, the goal is to create an immersive brand experience that aligns with your platform, creates a unique and compelling experience for your audience, and serves your business operations efficiently. These considerations are especially important for brands that function in retail spaces, but they should be applied to work environments as well. Depending on the scope of your brand environment project, you may consider working with an architect, interior designer, or retail designer in addition to the design consultants or agency you hired for your brand launch.

"You should be able to cover up the logo and still identify the company because the look and feel is so distinctive."

—*Michael Bierut, quoted from Alina Wheeler's* Designing Brand Identity

Integrating Brand Elements

As with all other branded materials, your environment will reflect the values of your brand. Imagine walking into an Apple retail store in which all logos have been removed. Which elements in that space would remind you that you are still in an Apple store? Each element you include in your environment will require careful consideration of functionality, durability, and emotional influence. We recommend working with your design team to create a mood board with examples of material, color, influential styles, and functional and decorative elements. This will help you feel and communicate the type of environment you envision. Once your environmental essence is established, your design team will be able to incorporate concrete items such as architecture, paint, signage, wall decor, furniture, lighting, and even smell to support your brand.

TRADITIONAL AND ESSENTIAL COLLATERAL

Every new brand requires outreach materials to support and promote business growth. Regardless of the specific collateral you choose to craft with your creative partners, each piece should be able to stand alone and function seamlessly alongside your other branded materials.

For your initial brand launch, we recommend having the following essentials on hand: business cards, letterhead (digital), note cards, fax template, and e-mail signatures.

Business cards: The business card is often the first means of introduction in social settings, so it needs to take advantage of what LinkedIn and company websites cannot do. A business card can create a lasting personal impression through sophisticated and innovative design, paper stock, and concept. You will immediately gain respect if you share a well-crafted and impressive business card with prospective business partners and clients.

Photography by Jason Ware

Most successful business cards combine a creative concept, compelling design, quality material, and custom printing to achieve memorability. The following is a list of custom printing options you may want to discuss with your creative partner:

Spot Varnish: translucent gloss coating that can be applied to any area of the design

Metallic Ink: reflects light for a sophisticated look

Die Cutting: allows you to cut the card into a custom shape

Embossing: part of the design that is raised from the flat surface of the paper

Debossing: part of the design that is impressed into the surface of the paper

Unconventional material such as plastic, metal, or wood: requires a specialized printer

With all of these printing options, you can easily remain true to your brand's core values and design strategy; don't get carried away by too many effects unless they add to the whole Brand Atmosphere.

Correspondence materials: When you exchange formal information with business partners and clients, custom-designed brand templates go a long way in upholding a professional and consistent brand image. Use templates for letterhead, contracts, official forms, and envelope design. You may want to include the same basic information from your business cards on each template as well. See the next page for an example of a cohesive collateral set we designed for Match Creative Talent.

E-mail signature: It's rarely given much thought in brand creation or marketing efforts, but your e-mail signature may be seen by hundreds of eyeballs on a daily basis. Once you start thinking of this rather minuscule part of your communications a little more strategically, you will see how it can easily turn into an important branding tool with a built-in and engaged audience—a tool that is personal and, yes, free.

Your signature can further engage current clients and partners or educate potential clients and employees about your brand's mission and culture. Working with entrepreneurs day in and day out, we always stress the signature as the simplest, yet most overlooked, brand asset. Usually it is greeted by a deer-in-the-headlights type of aha moment, one that we would love to project onto you by sharing five incredibly easy ways to push your brand upwards, while sending your e-mails outwards:

- **Never use your logo in your e-mail signature:** Naturally we have a desire to showcase our brand identity design (the logo) in our signature. Given that we run a brand consultancy, it might catch

LET'S TAKE THIS CONVERSATION OFFLINE

Offline is special today because, in this digital age, it is different. It is tangible and memorable. You don't "like" but actually truly enjoy a brand. Instead of hitting "share" the way you hit snooze on your alarm clock, you have a real conversation with people who trust you about a brand. Now that we are all well versed in pay-per-click ads and (finally) social media, it is time to hit the pause button and think about what it is that makes your brand special and the best way to engage with your audience in your outreach efforts. How will you create memorable, perhaps even inventive, inspirational campaigns? Some may be online like in 2015, but some should be offline like in 2016 (or 2006). The best place to look for inspiration is in the most offline of places: bars. Firestone Walker's beer coasters (pictured above) are completely on-brand while also starting a clever conversation about defending one's beer. Traditional marketing can be seen as a novelty today, and if you treat it uniquely and match it with the core values and personality of your brand, you might agree that retro is the new now and offline is the new online, even for your digital-first brand. So when you gear up for your marketing outreach, perhaps go single-gear and stand out instead.

Photography by: Fabian Geyrhalter

you even more by surprise that we advise against using your logo in your signature. But depending on technicalities at yours or the receiver's end, that logo may only show up as an attachment. When your recipient sees two attachments but only one document, it is a surefire way to confuse her—not a good message to send and surely not a great way to build your brand. Instead, use generic HTML fonts to mimic your logo's color scheme and, if applicable, its type treatment (see example on the opposite page). It won't be your logo, but it will resemble your Brand Atmosphere. Your correspondents will see it and know it's authentically your brand.

- **Resurface or repurpose your tagline:** The tagline used to be one of the key brand communication tools. Times have changed; today, taglines often end up being the headline on your landing page or used only in certain lock-ups of your logo. It's time to celebrate your tagline again. It is a clever elevator pitch in a few words that quickly describes your brand's purpose. The e-mail is the perfect piece in your marketing mix for it to appear, be shared, and live happily ever after.

- **Showcase all of your brand's active social media channels:** This one's a no-brainer. Check your signature and update it to make sure that all social brand channels are showcased, as there are new ones popping up faster than you can read this chapter. There is no easier way to gain followers who care. Period.

- **Leave them with your genuine thoughts, not a dead man's quote:** People are over the inspirational quotes, and they don't need to know your message was sent using your iPhone, tablet, or smartwatch. Instead, use your signature real estate to highlight the latest blog post you wrote or share interesting news of your brand—yet another way to create additional touch points. Remember that you already have the attention of a reader, and she is only one click away from learning more about your brand. The "leadership area" of your signature, as we like to call it, can be individualized by department or receiver, too. This can ensure that the information is personal and relevant.

- **The more parts to your signature, the more important design becomes:** When all is said and done, ensure your signature is not overwhelming. It needs to always be the second read after your message, even when you reply to an e-mail with just the two letters "OK." The signature should always feel just like that: a place to either grab a phone number or address from or to further engage with your brand. By implementing these tips, you will now have successfully achieved the latter.

Example of such e-mail signature:

Fabian Geyrhalter Principal

FINIEN

TURNING VENTURES INTO BRANDS

562-432-7627
320 Pine Ave, Suite 1010, Long Beach, CA 90802

JANUARY 21 - New Brand Post
Re-think Your Elevator Pitch: How To Successfully Introduce Your Brand In Conversation

THE #1 AMAZON BESTSELLER - How To Launch a Brand

Site | Twitter | Blog | Facebook | LinkedIn | Clarity

ADDITIONAL COLLATERAL
DEPENDING ON YOUR BRAND'S NEEDS

keynote/powerpoint presentation
email/newsletter templates
signage (outdoor/indoor)
advertisements
brochures/pamphlets
banners/posters
trade-show displays
trade-show giveaways
packaging
press kits
white papers
annual reports
manuals
furniture
menus
uniforms/t-shirts
vehicles
videos
mailing labels

BRAND ATMOSPHERE TOUCH POINTS:
Takeaways & Insights

+ Cohesive/Holistic/Systematic: Call it what you want. Your brand and all of the elements that make up your brand need to visually speak the same language and communicate the same message. It will make or break a Brand Atmosphere.

+ Don't try to be on all social media platforms at the outset. Strategize where it is most relevant for your brand to exist and apply a cohesive look-and-feel and brand voice to those channels first. You can always expand to other channels as time allows and needs arise.

+ Focus on just a few select traditional marketing pieces to get your brand started. Ensure that these pieces communicate the essence of your brand and are well designed.

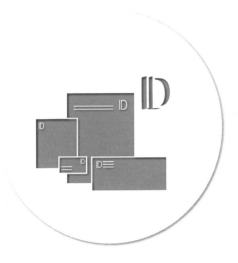

+ Each touch point associated with your brand has the power to diminish or enhance your Brand Atmosphere. Never rush through creating your touch points, and do sweat the small stuff.

References

Adams, S., Morioka, N., & Stone, T. (2004). *Logo Design Workbook: A Hands-On Guide to Creating Logos*. China: Rockport Publishers.

Airey, D. (2010). *Logo design love: a guide to creating iconic brand identities*. Berkeley, CA: New Riders.

Berger, W. (2013, March). Forget the mission statement. What's your mission question? Fast Co. Design. Retrieved from http://www.fastcodesign.com/1672137/forget-the-mission-statement-whats-your-mission-question

Bonezzi, A. (2009, Nov. 1). Name-letter branding: How your name can influence your choices.Retrieved June 15, 2013 from: http://insight.kellogg.northwestern.edu/article/name-letter_branding

Coleman, C. (2013, April 11). How to create a workplace people never want to leave. Bloomberg Business Week. Retrieved from http://www.businessweek.com/articles/2013-04-11/how-to-create-a-workplace-people-never-want-to-leave-by-googles-christopher-coleman

Daye, D. (2012). Brand positioning: Selecting a point of difference. Brand Strategy Insider. Retrieved from http://www.brandingstrategyinsider.com/2012/04/brand-positioning-selecting-a-point-of-difference.html#.UXWns4IhydM

Field, B. (2011, Feb.) Business plan: Your unique selling proposition. [Video file]. Retrieved from https://www.youtube.com/user/SmallBusinessBC

Fleisher, C., & Bensoussan, B. (2007). *Business and competitive analysis: Effective application of new and classical methods*. Upper Saddle River, NJ: FT Press.

Halvorson, K. (2008, Dec. 16). The discipline of content strategy. Retrieved from http://alistapart.com/article/thedisciplineofcontentstrategy

Khalsa, D. S. & Stauth, C. (1999). *Brain Longevity: The breakthrough medical program that improves your mind and memory*. New York, NY: Grand Central Publishing.

King, S. (2002). *On writing: A memoir of the craft*. New York, NY: Pocket Books.

Lindstrom, M. (2005). *Brand sense: Sensory secrets behind the stuff we buy*. New York, NY: Free Press.

Maslow, A. (2013). *A theory of human motivation*. Tree of Knowledge Publishing.

Minayama, H. (2007). *World branding: Concept, strategy, and design*. Corte Madera, CA: Gingko Press Inc.

Moore, G. (2006). *Crossing the chasm: Marketing and selling disruptive products to mainstream customers*. New York, NY: Harper Collins Publishers.

Morville, P., & Rosenfeld, L. (2007). *Information architecture for the world wide web*. Sebastopol, CA: O'Reilly.

O'Neill, S. (2009, Sept. 24). Travel innovators we love: Adam Wells. Retrieved from: http://www.budgettravel.com/blog/travel-innovators-we-love-adam-wells,10851/

Parallax Scrolling. (n.d.). Retrieved May, 2013 from http://en.wikipedia.org/wiki/Parallax_scrolling

Patagonia Inc. (2013). Our reason for being. Retrieved from: http://www.patagonia.com/us/patagonia.go?assetid=2047&ln=140

Responsive Web Design. (n.d.). Retrieved May, 2013 from http://en.wikipedia.org/wiki/Responsive_web_design

Ross, M. (2010). *Branding basics for small businesses: How to create an irresistible brand on any budget*. Nashville, IN: NorLightsPress.com.

Schwab, S (2011, March 31). Finding Your Brand Voice. Retrieved from: http://www.socialmediaexplorer.com/social-media-marketing/finding-your-brand-voice/

Sinek, S. (2010, May). Simon Sinek: How great leaders inspire action [Video file]. Retrieved from https://www.ted.com/talks/simon_sinek_how_great_leaders_inspire_action.html

Tunguz, T. (2013, March 13). Why Branding Is the Next Essential Startup Competency. Retrieved from: http://tomtunguz.com/branding

Virgin America Launches the 'Experience' Campaign with the Help of its Frequent Flyers. (2012, Sept. 5). Retrieved from: http://www.virginamerica.com/press-release/2012/virgin-america-experience-campaign.html

Walshe, P. (2012). Unlocking key traits for success and value. Millward Brown. Retrieved from: http://www.millwardbrown.com/BrandZ/Top_100_Global_Brands/Brand_Personality.aspx

Wharton School of the University of Pennsylvania. (2002, July 17). What's In a Name? Not Much Without a Branding Strategy. Retrieved from: http://knowledge.wharton. upenn.edu/article.cfm?articleid=593

Wheeler, A. (2013) *Designing brand identity: An essential guide for the whole branding team.* Hoboken, NJ: John Wiley & Sons, Inc.

Index

About Fabian Geyrhalter

Fabian Geyrhalter is the Founder and Principal of FINIEN.

Geyrhalter has been published internationally by the likes of the *Washington Post*, *Graphis*, and *Communication Arts*. He has written about branding for publications including *Mashable* and *Entrepreneur* and is a columnist for *Inc.*

Photography by: Dan Busta

An active jury member of the Academy of Interactive and Visual Arts and the winner of numerous design awards, including twenty-eight American Graphic Design Awards, Geyrhalter is often invited to judge international design competitions. He served as an adjunct professor at USC and Art Center College of Design and is an advisory board member for Santa Monica College. Geyrhalter is a frequent speaker and mentor to entrepreneurs worldwide and a "Global 100" mentor at the Founder Institute.

For twelve years he has been running the highly successful branding and graphic design agency Geyrhalter & Co., working for clients such as the Bill & Melinda Gates Foundation, Goodwill, Brandman University, W Hotels, CO-OP Financial Services, USC, Evolution Juice, the City of Los Angeles, and John Varvatos.

Geyrhalter was born in Vienna, Austria, and is a graduate of Art Center College of Design.

For brand launch or consulting engagements, speaking inquiries, or comments about How to Launch a Brand, *please contact Fabian Geyrhalter at fgeyrhalter@finien.com. For assistance with specific brand pain points and questions, Fabian can be reached for swift and insightful phone consultations via clarity.fm/fabiangeyrhalter.*

About FINIEN

FINIEN is a Los Angeles-based consultancy that turns ventures into brands. Our focus is narrow and our process specific. Our expertise is deep and our passion contagious. Collaboratively we embark on a short and intense journey to infuse new products and services with soul and an elevated reason for being. One that transforms companies—intellectually, verbally, and visually—into brands that will stand out and quickly and deeply resonate with customers from the get-go.

Branding Insights

Enjoyed the book? Fabian Geyrhalter regularly publishes new thought pieces on branding. Sign up to receive his latest insights free in your inbox via **tinyurl.com/finiensignup**

Acknowledgements

A debt of gratitude to **Leah E. Bisch**, **Marissa Hui**, and **Courtney Hyde** for their dedication to and enthusiasm for this special FINIEN project.

Special thanks to Division 4 Group (Vienna, Austria) for the ongoing support in Europe.

Key typefaces used throughout this book:
DIN by Albert-Jan Pool and Open Sans by Steve Matteson

Design by FINIEN.

Lightning Source UK Ltd.
Milton Keynes UK
UKRC01n1904100817
307101UK00001B/14

* 9 7 8 0 9 8 9 6 4 6 1 3 0 *